NOT PERFECTLY DIVIDED

Unity! The Road to Justice and Equality

By

Fred Easter

NOT PERFECTLY DIVIDED

© 2021 Fred Easter

Cover Design: Fred Easter

Editor: F. Scott Bradford

Graphic Artist: Bennie Thompson

Sketch Artist: Johnathan Thompson

Consultant: Darren Wilson

Fred Easter Publications

CONTENTS

CHAPTER I: DIVIDED COUNTRY

*	The Coronavirus	1
*	Three Branches of Government	2–4
*	America's Beginning	4–5
*	Contributions of All Americans	6–9
*	The Biggest Con	10–12
*	The Right Path to Equality	12–14
*	Vote or Sink	14–23
*	Unforgettable Lesson	23–24
*	Ahmaud Arbery Couldn't Jog and Live	24–26
*	We Already Have the Road Map for Equality and Justice, LET'S USE IT	26–29
*	Key Elements Needed for Our Wealth and Power	29–30
*	Education Is a Must	30–33
*	There's No Connection without Communication	33–34
*	The Importance of Values	34–37
*	The Power of Pain and Fear	37–38
*	Respect	38
*	My Drug Use	38–44
*	The Knee on George Floyd's Neck	44–45
*	Police Kill Breonna Taylor While She Sleeps	45–48
*	The Protest	48–50

CHAPTER II: GLOBAL DIVIDE

*	A Global Divide Has Worsened This Pandemic	51–64
*	Modern Day Slavery	64–67

CHAPTER III: COMMUNITY DIVIDE

*	Community Divide	69–75
*	Social Programs	75–84
*	Healthcare	84–89
*	School Busing	89–90
*	Advantages of Eliminating Busing	90–91
*	Advantages of School Busing	91–92
*	The Division Caused by Drugs	92–96
*	Prescription Drugs and Alcohol	97–99

CHAPTER IV: RELIGIOUS DIVIDE

*	Man Created Religion	101
*	The Struggle	102–103
*	God Has No Religion or Gender	103–104
*	My Position	104–105
*	Church Rules	105–106
*	The Playground	106–112
*	Different Prayers to One God	112–114
*	Church & State: Not Close	114–115

CHAPTER V: POLITICAL DIVIDE

*	The Soul of the Nation	117–120
*	Distinguishing the Truth Is Not an Option	120–124
*	Government Decisions Can Be Deadly and Lasting	124–133
*	Gangster in the White House Surrounded by His Hitmen	134–135

CHAPTER VI: GENDER DIVIDE

*	Understanding Strength and Weakness	137-141
*	The Hardest Job: A Mother	141-147
*	Women Sacrificed All the Way to the Grave	147-153
*	LGBTQ and Trans Citizens Feel the Heat	153-159
*	Another Glass Ceiling Shattered	159-164

CHAPTER VII: THE POWER OF SPORTS IN POLITICS

*	Politics and Sports	165–172

CHAPTER VIII: DIVIDED FAMILIES

*	The Weakness Caused by the Divide	173
*	Unknown Connections	173–178

*	Family Research	178–179
*	My Mother Was Born a Ward	179–180
*	Meet Me in St. Louis	180–181
*	The Family	181–182
*	Can the Family Stay Together	182–185
*	The Move and the Reconnection	185–188
*	The Marriage	189–192

CHAPTER IX:
FAMILY CHALLENGES

*	The Northside	193–198
*	The Eighth Grade	198–202
*	Denver Colorado	202–207
*	Drugs Weren't Finished with Me	207–210
*	A Brand New Me	211–213
*	The Entrepreneur	213–220
*	Reparations Begin with Families	220–221
*	My Greatest Appreciation	221–224

CONCLUSION   225–226

PHOTOS   227–236

REFERENCES   237–245

DEDICATION

Every word I write is dedicated to families all over the world that have lost loved ones due to hate and systemic racism. I write with the hope that, through

UNITY,

their deaths will **<u>not</u>** be

IN VAIN

ACKNOWLEDGMENTS

I realize that I have an awful lot to be thankful for and multitudes of people to be thankful to. This list of people is inclusive of those who served as inspirations or provided hands-on guidance and assistance at every step in my writing.

Mario Hampton, Carlos Michael McIntosh, Stanley Williams, Donald Gunn and Aretha Fultz are all good friends of mine who gave me encouragement. Lisa Allen, mother of my daughter Rukiya, was also instrumental. Special thanks to my nephew, Cory Davis, who passed years ago. There is a need for me to mention TRG an organization headed by my good friend Gene Gordon that I give a shout out to. I must also mention all of those from the Penrose neighborhood who have passed on to another plane. You were all with me as I told these stories. Likewise, special thanks to my cousin, Gerald Easter, who has passed away.

Floyd Allen has shown his unselfish support in bringing this book to life. I'd also like to thank my attorneys Robin Desmond and Fernando Freyre. Big thanks to Aretha Franklin, the greatest soul singer of all time, whose voice was there with every word I wrote. I also thank my eighth-grade teacher, Dr. Billie Mayo, who was the initial inspiration for me to write.

Another thanks to Bob Marley for the vision in

his song *Get Up, Stand Up*. No, we can't give up the fight.

I recall seeing Cedric The Entertainer visiting relatives on Lee Avenue. This local comedian never forgot his roots and has made countless contributions to his hometown, so thanks to my fellow St. Louisan for keeping it real in the best possible sense.

A special shout out to Dick Gregory, who I have never met, but who was born and raised in St. Louis and touched the heart, soul and spirit of activism in the people here.

I also feel the need to give a shout-out to some of the young entertainers and activists speaking up for the cause. That includes Jay Z and Beyoncé, who remain engaged in their efforts to fight for justice and equality.

I would be remiss not to mention Lebron James, who continuously uses his wealth and influence to make a positive change.

I give a special thanks to Narcotics Anonymous (NA) and Alcoholics Anonymous (AA), who have been instrumental in helping addicts all over the world in their recovery.

Special thanks to three of my brothers who are no longer with us in the flesh, but whose stories grace these pages: Daryl Steele, Charles James Easter and Joseph Easter El. Likewise, my grandmother Francis Ward; my mother, Marie Easter; and my father, Julius Easter live on in these pages. Even though they've left this plane, I still stand on their shoulders.

My brother Harry Easter and my sister-cousin, Mary Davis have helped me every step of the way with the writing of this book.

At this time, I'm driven to give a special acknowledgement to the children of my wife, Willie Spruill, Regina Spruill, Kimberly Spruill, Tammie Spruill and her grandchildren Amin, Willie, Bryan and Chris who have accepted me so warm and graciously into their lives.

Special thanks to my daughter Rukiya Pargo; my son-in-law Ivan Pargo; my granddaughters Raven, Kamryn, and Maddison and my great-grandson, Chase.

Finally, I would like to thank my wife Ameriles Easter. Without her, I wouldn't have started this book and I certainly couldn't have finished it. Her support has been unequaled and endless, day-in and day-out. Thank you again and again.

INTRODUCTION

Even though inspiration is elusive in nature, when it strikes, it can awaken us to tremendous possibilities that would otherwise lie dormant. Such inspiration is often born of necessity, from observing situations that must change or need improvement.

As an African American man born and raised in St. Louis, Missouri, I have a deep understanding of how systemic racism can distort the opportunities a city provides. I've witnessed bitter battles between neighbors, police officers, even family members in my lifetime. That strife has created in me a strong desire to right some basic wrongs we have come to accept. There were a series of traumatic incidents in my life that contributed to the person I am today. I share some of these stories with you in the hopes that my experiences can expand your world view. I hope my life story lives with you in a way that helps you think more deeply about this world that we all share, and perhaps helps you draw some conclusions that you might not have otherwise reached.

St. Louis is home to some of the most divided and violent communities in the country. This rebellious behavior in my people is no coincidence, but rather the direct result of centuries of systemic racism that continues to fester and breed hate. That behavior was at the root of one of the most transformative experiences of my childhood.

"Pow, pow, pow!" I still remember the shots that rang out as we were preparing to leave my elementary school.

"Get down, get down! Hit the ground!" one kid shouted.

All of us followed these urgent instructions as we quickly dove to the concrete pavement in total fear, hoping not to be killed by flying bullets that seemed to target everyone and no one in particular.

"Stay down, just stay down," he said, over and over until after several minutes he slowly and cautiously lifted himself up from the ground. This kid continued to survey the streets and all passing cars as if he were a military captain waiting to give his troops further instruction. The kids began to get up—some running away while others stood by in complete disbelief, moaning and complaining about how tired they were of having to go through this all too often, as if once wasn't too much.

Even though this happened during wartime in the Vietnam era, these combat maneuvers took place at Scullin Elementary School in St. Louis, Missouri. The youngster barking out orders to the other kids was a child himself, only about eleven or twelve years of age. Through no fault of his own, he had become accustomed to the gun violence that was ravaging our communities. I was one of the kids diving to the pavement to avoid being shot by someone I likely didn't even know. At the time, these tragedies almost seemed normal, expected even. When I look back on it, I realize that these incidents were part of a slow indoctrination into a life of low expectations that too many of us were conditioned to accept.

This senseless flurry of gunshots turned out to be the work of teenagers from the Newstead neighborhood a few blocks away. The constant fighting and attacks on one another were routine and left a continual cloud of fear over our entire community. The sad thing is, I didn't know a single person who knew the reason for the constant fighting. To this day, I'm not positive I have a better understanding of our hate for one another. I've come to believe that this hate has evolved in us through unconscious training, crushing poverty and low standards that suffocate the development of hopes and dreams.

As often as these incidents occurred, I was never questioned or reassured by the police, nor do I recall any of my classmates being questioned or comforted. The complete absence of a police presence was evidence of the fact that institutionally, our local police organizations had long past given up on the community they were supposed to assist. Instead of looking to our police to "protect and serve," our neighborhood lived under the premise of "watch, detain and enforce," the same philosophy that ruled so cruelly in times of slavery. This is not an indictment of all police, but rather an indictment of the systems that were designed and evolved as relics of an earlier and openly white supremacist era. These systems in which so many good men and women serve honorably, continue to function institutionally in ways that horrify police and punish poor communities of color rather than aid or serve them. The presumption of inferiority at the root of these old policies are undermining the very reasons many fine young men and women joined the force.

My experiences growing up in an African American neighborhood were not unique. As a matter of fact, this was the norm throughout America. This system of intermittently absent or aggressive policing, along with so many other systemic paths of disenfranchisement, are why we live today in a world of protest, rioting and looting, lacking the ability to come together even to curb the death toll of COVID-19. As this disease continues to ravage us, we're now forced to deal simultaneously with social crises that have been building for centuries as we demand recognition of our civil and human rights.

The fact that African Americans and other minorities are still fighting to end unjust systemic treatment is only confirmation of how resistant and powerful the opposition remains. Despite centuries of demagoguery, injustice and downright brutal beat downs of my people—physically, mentally, socially and in every way possible—the need to maintain a concept of white superiority, the sheer resilience of race-based oppression, still carries momentum. That is why I am so proud of our young people, from all walks of life and of all nationalities, who led a powerful global response against racial violence in 2020.

It's hard to imagine that the race toward true and lasting change championed by our greatest freedom fighters, Harriet Tubman, Nat Turner, Frederick Douglass, Sojourner Truth, the Reverend Dr. Martin Luther King Jr., John Lewis and others, continues uphill in 2020 despite their sacrifices. More recent warriors, like Huey P. Newton, Bobby Seale, Noble Drew Ali, Marcus Garvey, Elijah Muhammad and the Minister Louis Farrakhan, continued the struggle through another era. I'm sure it would bring joy to all the aforementioned to realize that their fearlessness and determination lives on today in groups like Black Lives Matter.

Support from allies outside of the Black community has always existed and has always been needed and much appreciated. However, what we witnessed over the summer of 2020 was absolutely unprecedented. This rising tide of support from people of all colors, from all nations, taking to the streets in waves and waves of solidarity for Black lives was breathtaking. I was transfixed by the Black Lives Matter protests happening all over our country and abroad, all summer. This movement, after so many centuries, has in my estimation finally achieved critical mass. The movement is unstoppable as long as we're not distracted by the forces that will undoubtedly attempt to sabotage and sew distrust and confusion among the ranks of activists and their supporters.

There have already been multiple reports of infiltrations at Black Lives Matter rallies by militant hate groups such as the KKK and other White supremacist groups. Some have been caught on video smashing windows and inciting riots while pretending to be members of the Black Lives Matter movement. After the murder of George Floyd, one of the rioters identified in the aftermath was the infamous "umbrella man" with known ties to the Hell's Angels and White supremacist groups like the Aryan Cowboys. He earned this name by holding an umbrella over his head to hide his identity while committing acts of destruction, as nearby protestors peacefully exercised their First Amendment rights. The young people fighting for justice will not be so easily scapegoated or give up, and neither will I.

Let's not be confused—this struggle is not just about George Floyd or any other single individual. It's a universal battle for the heart and soul of people all over the world. The global powers that be have already claimed ownership to everything of value on earth and on the moon by planting their flags and laying stake. What's left to own? If issues of inequality are not addressed now, they will follow us into new industries, new healthcare systems, even new colonies as we look beyond the earth and our devastated planet. The same architects of greed and destruction that have laid waste to our brilliant planet might one day deliver their most vile export to another world.

  I know you're probably thinking that I'm getting ahead of myself, but nearsightedness has become one of the movement's greatest stumbling blocks. Furthermore, if we don't reverse course soon on our crushing level of inequality, all of us, rich and poor alike, will share a similar fate. The course we're on now is simply not sustainable. We have to move forward with an eye toward establishing a baseline of worth and dignity for everyone or we will perish together.

  Through my writing, I hope to give the world a microscopic view into the problems that poor communities face and offer some solutions that will strike a blow against the type of abject poverty that destroys neighborhoods and people. We'll especially look at neighborhoods further crippled by systemic racism. The absence of resources in these neighborhoods affects us more than we realize. We've just become accustomed to living with the fallout. We people of color tend to normalize our mistreatment and accept it as the natural order. Poor education, inadequate healthcare, differentials in pay, housing discrimination, unfair treatment from banks and other lending institutions are just a few examples of the systemic racism that alter the arc of our potential.

Add to that unfair treatment due to religious beliefs, gender discrimination, and police brutality and you get the full picture of the obstacles people in these communities can face. When we throw the police into this mix of systemic failures, we see how quickly the goal to protect and serve can devolve into a mission to contain the collateral damage. It doesn't help that the few bad cops who enter this mix interpret their mission without mercy or compassion for the people they serve. They set out to stop, detain and confront constituents they view as the problem, not as the community. If we're honest, the police have been placed in a no-win situation, which makes them just as much victims of these systemic failures as you and me.

CHAPTER I:
DIVIDED COUNTRY

THE CORONAVIRUS

The pictures coming out of New York City this spring were grim. Lines of tractor trailers in service as temporary morgues flanked hospitals overwhelmed by the biggest health catastrophe since the Spanish flu pandemic of 1918.

We became accustomed to the pictures of hospital workers, still draped in PPE, seeking some temporary respite in the out of doors from the relentless sound and chaos of the ICU. We would watch them on our screens, sitting head in hands, praying, crying or simply looking lost.

Human beings are divisive by nature, in every way possible. We see the results of our division through war, gang violence, and general disregard for our fellow man. The Coronavirus may not have been preventable, but because of our current state of disconnect, this virus has quickly brought our nation to its knees. We would not have dreamed it was possible. We are now afraid to go to the store, walk the beach, or send our kids to school. We won't even shake hands to greet our fellow man. We, as a country, are now prepared to spend trillions to tackle this beast of a virus for fear that it will overtake our society completely, and it is well on the way to doing just that if we don't come together.

THREE BRANCHES OF GOVERNMENT

When the country's founders devised three co-equal branches of government, they hoped to create a balance of powers that would enshrine fairness and an equal playing field for those considered worthy. Being a Black man, I would not have made the cut. I have a few choice words to offer on the original American ideal of fairness, but we'll get to that a little later.

Our three branches of government, executive, legislative and judicial, were meant to hold the line against any tyrants who might arise to challenge our fledgling new republic. We can now safely say that at least some of our elected officials have fully abandoned their commitment to that ideal in support of a president who is exactly the bad actor the founders feared. On top of that, the money in politics is completely hijacking the people's business. Most of our appointed officials can't come together on anything outside of their own self-interest. The money that we spend on elections, from the local level to the presidency, is horrifying. Ask yourself—how can any position not be corrupt when there is so much money required to have and hold the position, and so much money thrown about by corrupt people to keep it?

The test of the last four years has been to determine if our system can survive a true challenge in the presidency of one Donald J.

Trump. His entire life has been lived with the sole purpose of obtaining wealth and power. In his greed, he has always stepped on the dreams of the constituents he's cheated and encouraged hate with his unsubstantiated rhetoric. He has shown us repeatedly exactly who he is. To take a quote from the great and wise Maya Angelou, "When someone shows you who they are, believe them."

I don't want anyone to think that I'm laying blame at the feet of Donald J. Trump, because nothing could be further from the truth. Yes, he has done all that he has been allowed to do to further division and sew hate, but he is only one of many vehicles driving down this path.

There is more than enough blame to go around for how this great and powerful country has failed so many so often. The Congress has always had its share of flaws. That's understandable. No system is perfect. But the place we find our leaders in now is rooted in hate, greed and a complete lack of empathy for the average American. The Blues against the Grays! Yes, I said it. We are witnessing a modern-day civil war with soldiers dressed up in suits and ties and armed with fancy words that only serve to deepen the divide. Shame on you!

I don't want anyone to be confused by my message because this is far too serious a subject for a country that stands on the precipice of a deep and irreversible divide. I will not allow my voice to make matters worse, but I write knowing that as a nation we must be able to handle the truth. I can only hope that my words can touch some hearts and minds that will help make a difference. There are a lot of good people in positions of leadership in this country, and those people will continue to fight for what is right. Some will be compromised, too. To pursue what is right with integrity sounds so simple, but in a system vulnerable to big money corruption it is certainly not easy.

Allow me to take you on a journey in time, for the purpose of giving us all a better understanding of how the divide in this country and all countries, began.

AMERICA'S BEGINNING

The American Revolution began in 1775 and ended in 1783. America's first thirteen colonies gained independence from Great Britain after a long and bloody war. On September 9th, 1776, the Continental Congress officially declared the new nation the United States of America, no longer the United Colonies.

Each of the colonies was settled by people from different regions of England, all with different accents and marital and dating customs. They even dressed differently and worshipped in their own churches. Some of their ancestors had been European indentured servants working under contract. Once their contracts were fulfilled, they were afforded the opportunity to work their own land and accumulate wealth the best way that they knew how, through tobacco. The crop was in great demand with remarkable profits as an export commodity. This would require hard work and a lot of it. This is where my people, the so-called "African American", came into the picture. I refer to us as so-called African Americans because the last time I checked Africa was a continent, and no nationality can be derived from a continent, regardless of how great it is.

In August of 1619, Africans arrived on the shores of Virginia. The influx of Africans reached its highest peak after the thirteen colonies achieved independence. We were a hardworking people, and we worked from sunup till sundown, building riches for those that enslaved us. The divide that derived from us being taken from our homeland was only the beginning of the great division that still exists today. We were separated from our families of origin, children were separated from their parents, and through this we were separated from our culture as well.

The hard work that we performed for this nation was unending, even though there was no reward for our services. There is nothing wrong with hard work, but hard work that begets more work and no wealth is un-American to the core.

Not Perfectly Divided

CONTRIBUTIONS OF ALL AMERICANS

African Americans have made so many contributions to the wealth and growth of this country that it would be impossible to list them all in a single chapter.

The cotton planter and the seed planter were both invented by Henry Blair. The magnificent lady that escorted more than 300 slaves to freedom, one Harriet Ross Tubman, gifted Black women with an example of hard work and activism that endures. And let's not forget George Washington Carver, the agriculturalist inventor of more than three hundred peanut products. Thomas L. Jennings was the inventor of dry cleaning. The world of music would not be the same today without greats like Muddy Waters, Barry Gordy, Mahalia Jackson and the greatest soul singer of all time, Aretha Franklin. It would be remiss of me not to mention a lady that was born and raised in my own hometown of St. Louis, Missouri, the relentless fighter for justice, California Representative Maxine Waters.

I could go on and on about the accomplishments of my people, but I want to share with you some of the great things that other nationalities contributed to this great country of ours, to help transform it into a place that we all can be proud to call the home of the brave.

The railroad, the sewer system and even the canals that have become so vital for our well-being would not exist without the hard work and expertise of the Irish. They even played a major role in the building of some of the most fantastic skyscrapers. They helped build the highways and bridges and developed American infrastructure. And let's not forget the many contributions that they made in sports and entertainment. Joseph P. Kennedy was an American businessman that played a major role in our political world. Not to mention that he was the force behind his sons Robert, Ted, and John F. Kennedy, the thirty-fifth president of these United States of America.

Germans came to the United States to escape poor economic conditions, political oppression and religious persecution. Like immigrants before and after them, they came to have a better life. Nearly 8 million Germans migrated to America between 1820 and 1870, accounting for more than 40 million descendants. Germans contributed in so many ways that made a profound difference in our way of life here in the United States.

    The concept of kindergarten was imported to the states when Margarethe Schurz opened the first American "children's garden" for her Watertown, Wisconsin community in 1856. German engineer John Roebling built our famous and much-loved Brooklyn Bridge. The Christmas tree and the presents that come with it were introduced to America by way of German culture. Frederick Trump, grandfather of Donald J. Trump, migrated to America, yet another president who came from a family of immigrants.

Between 1880 and 1924, more than 4 million Italians fled poverty from Southern Italy and Sicily, migrating to America with hopes and dreams of a better life and a brighter future for their families. The resulting Italian migration brought new food, art and music into American culture. The hard work of many Italians enhanced the growth of this country in a way that can't be fully measured or appreciated.

Godfather author Mario Puzo, singer and actor Frank Sinatra, the fifty-second Governor of the state of New York Mario Cuomo, his son Andrew Cuomo who now serves as governor are all Italian Americans. And let's not forget one of the most powerful women in the history of this country, Nancy Pelosi, the first woman Speaker of the House. She continues to fight the fight to help make this county a better and safer place to live.

There have been tremendous sacrifices for this nation by so many different people from all over the world. We are the lucky recipients of talents and intelligence from just about every country on the globe. And though it's impossible to list all of those nations here, to the immigrants who are beautifying our tapestry, you *are* appreciated.

I celebrate all the great people from different countries residing within our nation to emphasize our commonalities. The desire to enjoy and perfect our union should far outweigh our petty differences. We've created a rich new world that's unique on the planet. We would be foolish to allow our experiment to end because we've been manipulated to hate one another.

    Let's not forget who we are and why our forefathers from all over the world migrated here in the first place. It was for the sole purpose of having a better life, not to take their turn at inflicting the pain they were fleeing on the new arrivals. Some came to escape poverty, hunger and oppression while others, through no fault of their own, were forced to come to a foreign land to face fates worse than the ones they left. None of us, upon our initial arrival were welcomed, it's fair to say. For the most part, we were treated harshly as we patiently waited for our next generation to find their footing and make their way to the American dream.

    Some assimilated into this society with a smoother transition than others because their hue was more aligned with the existing powers—their opportunities as such more robust. Not that these paler immigrants were necessarily smarter or more productive. And though we ultimately tend to correct our bigotries, our memory is short. Each new immigrant group starts the struggle anew.

THE BIGGEST CON

The greatest distraction from the serious work that needs to be done to perfect our union for the millions of middle class and poverty-stricken people in these United States of America, are the bitter battles we wage against one another. We've been conned, bamboozled and made complete fools of for generations, and if we don't wise up, the con will continue for generations to come. Why do we continue to do this to ourselves? It just makes no sense to me.

Those of us that are blessed enough to be in overwhelming debt, look down our noses at those that are not fortunate enough to be in as much debt, as if this confirms our stature in the community. Pro-lifers and the pro-choice contingent have waged war against one another though we should all agree that an advanced wealthy nation should provide its smart, beautiful women with better options; gun owners hate anyone who can't abide military-grade weapons in unlimited supply within civil society; if the color of your skin is different, you'd better watch your back. And heaven of whatever stripe or shape help you if you practice a different religion, as some religious fanatics on the fringes feel entitled to harass, assault or kill you for the practice of your faith. Our LGBTQ neighbors are in constant danger just because they have chosen not to live a lie and have the courage to live their truth. We can't begin to count the many contributions made by gay, lesbian, bisexual and transgender people. Literally, we can't begin to count because so many for good reason remained in hiding.

While we little people continue to fight all these meaningless battles amongst ourselves and sink closer and closer to a state of obscurity and financial ruin, the rich and powerful continue to grow their wealth and enhance their iron-clad hold on our limited futures.

This is nothing new. This formula has been in effect for centuries and, at the rate that we are going, it will still be in effect for centuries to come. Our Black children and grandchildren deserve better than what we are in position to leave them; more debt than they will ever get out from under and no knowledge of how to create wealth and a brighter future for their existing families and their families to be.

What will we say to our children? "I didn't have the time to secure your financial future because I was busy fighting culture wars against other people that were being oppressed just like me? This is not fair to our children. It is our duty, as proud and loving parents, to pave the way by providing them a better opportunity than what was passed on to us. They shouldn't have the same fight that we still fight today, and our fathers fought before us.

When will we ever learn? Wealth, power

and prosperity does not come about accidentally, it comes only through wise decisions and a relentless pursuit of the true prize. We must pick our battles wisely and ensure we are advancing on the right fronts.

THE RIGHT PATH TO EQUALITY

We must stop giving away our power through division, and realize that we are in this fight together, and togetherness is the only way that positive changes for us will ever be made. We must put our petty differences aside and sit at our table of power, where real and productive changes can truly be made. It's not that hard if we can only be honest with ourselves and stop with the false pride and self-righteousness that only serves to blind us from ourselves and not allow us to see the future that we most certainly deserve.

Laws are put in place that allow the rich to stay rich and the poor to continue to stay poor. That's why we must take back our government and change the laws that are structured to disadvantage us in favor of corporations. We must stop being swindled into voting against our own best interest and spending the people's money on the rich man's priorities. What kind of sense does that make?

Let's start from scratch by identifying what is the most important factor that these elections are about, **WEALTH**. Everything else can, and will, be worked out in time, but we must start with the

WEALTH. Let's not get my position misconstrued—there have been and will always be a few exceptional people who will rise above the rest through the power of their inventiveness or intellect. Those people are a small fraction of the entire human population in the whole scheme of things. The only way to give all families an opportunity to create a brighter future, is to recognize and respect the contributions of the rest of us through fair wages, equal and guaranteed access to health care, education and basic social supports. Laws and good governance can make all these things happen. If we have the will and see the need, it's all quite possible. I know by now you're probably calling me a socialist. But let's not forget the billions of dollars that we shovel out to the rich and powerful continuously, from our paid taxes. These are the same people who continuously push the propaganda that government help is socialism. Not only do they rob our tax fund, but they then have the audacity to find loopholes to avoid paying their fair share to refill the coffers. Now *that's* a real "gravy train!"

The same money that they legally steal from our hard-earned taxes is then paid to lobbyists and politicians to guarantee that our laws continue to benefit them so the thievery and grift can continue. Those new laws passed for the benefit of the super wealthy only assure an even greater wealth divide. So in actuality, we are paying billions of dollars annually to support our poverty and we continue to vote these same politicians into office, over and over again. Let's hold these people accountable whether they're Republicans or Democrats and take our government back.

The only way to do this is by stripping this system down to its roots and taking the billions of dollars out of politics. The only way that someone can get elected now is through the aid of the filthy rich, and once elected, they become filthy too. I believe we had a true champion for the people in the race for the Democratic Presidential nomination in Elizabeth Warren, but she didn't get the nomination for several different reasons. A major reason being that the powers that be manufactured a polished propaganda campaign that was too much for her to overcome. That's because so many of us allow the money of the wealthy determine who gets our vote, instead of voting for our own best interest. I like to think that I'm a great judge of character and in my humble opinion Warren is smart, fearless and is truly on the side of what's right for *all* people.

VOTE OR SINK

There are plenty of other politicians that have their heart in the right place, and are very capable, but Warren is different. She knows **ECONOMICS**, and that makes her more than ready to tackle this great wealth divide that continues to cripple our country.

For any business to be successful the leader must have a great understanding of economics, and that she does. I only hope that if Joseph Biden or any other Democratic nominee is elected, they will not let the brilliance of this lady go to waste, but instead will give her their ear and put her in a position where she will be able to make a real difference. If they do, the American people won't regret it.

These upcoming elections in November of 2020 must surely be classified as one of the most important elections in this country's history and must be treated as such by all voters. If elected, Joseph Biden could prove to be a great President. In addition to his obvious empathy and devotion to fair play for the little guy, he has experience in so many areas of government that have prepared him for the great tasks ahead. The job will surely be difficult because of the mess that this present administration will leave behind. Biden must surround himself with the most qualified and dedicated people that this country has to offer; no butt kissers afraid to speak truth to power.

I'm not just advocating change in the presidential race. We need changes from the local, state and national levels of government through free and unsuppressed voting.

Do you believe what is happening with this coronavirus? Think about this, we have more than

Not Perfectly Divided

100,000 deaths in this country alone from this **BEAST**, and we are still counting. Does it have to affect each one of you directly for you to believe how serious it is? If you or someone very dear to you dies, then businesses being reopened soon will not benefit you at all. **WE MUST THINK FOR OURSELVES!**

If we just can't resist the urge to protest closings and restrictions, how about protesting for all these **NURSES, DOCTORS AND ESSENTIAL WORKERS** that put their lives on the line for all of us without the necessary equipment to protect their own lives. We stand up and cheer for them, we blow horns and make the buildings blue, as if this is appreciation enough. How about demanding that your President see to it that these people are protected and compensated for their heroic efforts.

If you or someone you know, have lost jobs and you can't afford to provide for your families, don't fret. There are millions of jobs available. We need people to administer tests for this virus, drivers and essential workers in so many more capacities, that I'm almost sure that you could be accommodated. If you choose to jump in the fight and be heroic, instead of standing on the sidelines complaining because you can't get a haircut, your country would appreciate your service.

You're right—I *am* mad as hell because we continue to demand more from those that have less. Our political leaders demonstrate daily that they don't give a damn about us, and they continue to get a pass. Donald J. Trump orders the meat factories to open back up without any additional protection for the workers making a living for their families. Is this slavery! ("*Get back out there in those fields and get that meat ready and thank me for ensuring that you still have a job through this crisis!*")

Mitch McConnell orders the Senate back, despite all the risk so he can vote in more conservative judges. To hell with all the emergencies facing the American people. He just wants to ensure his own selfish interests are fulfilled.

I share my heart and passion through this book, and I can only hope that I'm alive to see this project through, for I too am an essential worker. This heart and head of mine just desires to be heard. If through my words, someone has a change of heart and realizes just how connected we are and devotes themselves to promoting love and unity instead of division and hate, I'll consider that a win.

Enough about me, here comes the curve ball of the election season. Tara Reade steps up at the most inopportune time in Joseph Biden's election campaign with accusations of sexual harassment and sexual misconduct allegations from 1993.

I don't know if this happened or not, but he

has denied it unequivocally and has requested that these claims be investigated completely. That's in direct contrast to President Donald J. Trump, who has used all of his power to prohibit investigations for all of the criminal accusations that have been lodged against him—and there have been many—including more than a dozen sexual harassment and sexual misconduct allegations that have in some cases been supported by evidence and substantiated. But we continue to chase rabbits down every rabbit hole as it relates to the president's rivals.

This allegation against Joseph Biden is only the beginning of what will be a continuous and relentless onslaught. I'm sure we can scarcely imagine what lies in wait from Donald Trump and his allies as they attempt to dismantle Joseph Biden's campaign to retain their seat of power. The antics they dream up will surely rival the imagination of even the master storyteller, Steven Spielberg.

I truly believe that this country is at a crossroads and if we take the wrong path, we could tumble into a place of no redemption. I'm not professing to be a wise man or a prophet, I only know what I have witnessed, and that makes it crystal clear to me that this country is not nearly as divided as it will be. This President has proved to be a master of division, and that is his only path to ensuring another term in office. Let's not take him for granted again. If we do, this could truly prove to be catastrophic for the health, wealth and safety of people all over the world.

Donald J. Trump has methodically tapped into the emotions of hate and resentment in the confused minds of so many of his supporters. Even if legally voted out of office he could refuse to step down and disallow the usual transfer of power. If so, just his words alone could provoke an uprising that we would never have believed possible just four short years ago. I warn you all, this man will stop at nothing to avoid prosecution for the numerous crimes that he has committed while in office, and he knows that the leaders of the Democratic party, with possible control of the Senate and House, would pursue his convictions wholeheartedly.

The only way that I can Imagine Donald J. Trump not unleashing these rabid, cult like supporters, would be by assuring him that he and his family would not be prosecuted for any crimes. It's a damn shame that someone that has been fortunate enough to be granted this amazing amount of power, would be so selfish and reckless that he would misuse, deceive and continue to show disregard for the lives of so many, but he has already proven his viciousness.

This outright abdication of accountability we are witnessing in our Republican elected officials is certainly no accident. It tells us where the Grand

Ole Party stands. Their bargains for power have left them so compromised that there's no stopping this runaway train of greed—not even the engineers can jump off at this point. Meanwhile Donald Trump has taken over the train and he has no knowledge or understanding of what this job entails, nor does he care.

It appears that President Trump only wants to soak up as much of the wealth as possible, while Mitch McConnell continues to appoint right-wing judges and the remainder of the party continues to ingratiate themselves to Trump. They hope his approval of their dereliction of duty will garner them another term in the seat that they have already betrayed. The opportunity to disconnect from this madness was lost when these partisan Senators denied the people a vote for impeachment. Now we have Donald Trump, totally unrestrained to trample his underlings. They may not even have a chance to return to the you scratch my back, I'll scratch yours type of dealings.

Didn't any Republican learn from the thumbs down man, John McCain? Did the entire soul and integrity of the Republican party die when he took his last breath? I suppose so, because since his last stand there has been absolutely no resistance to Trump's flagrant disregard for democratic norms and the rule of law. I want you to understand that I disagreed with so much of what John McCain stood for and represented, but I respected his positions and I always respected him as a man and a patriot. There's nothing wrong with disagreement between people. In fact, I expect it and I appreciate it. Without it there would be no healthy dialogue and without dialogue there would be no growth or progress.

The few families that control most of our nation's wealth and power have always been very private and determined not to let any outsiders into their world. Despite his public persona as successful millionaire, Donald Trump is an outsider to this world. As such, his resentment and newfound power caused him to go rouge and search beyond our shores for the assistance of others who wield power and wealth in Russia, Saudi Arabia and who knows how many other countries.

These newfound relationships have allowed Trump and his cronies to disregard the nations that have historically been friends and allies of the United States, which has struck a blow to the normal world order and discouraged countries that were presumed allies of the United States. He is a very vengeful man with a long memory, which has proven to be destructive to say the least. He is also a narcissist looking for a world full of lackeys which he seems to have found in the GOP. A perfect fit for them but not for the rest of America.

Regardless of the disdain that I feel for this

man, I must acknowledge that he has made some decisions that were way overdue. The upcoming release of more than 3,000 prisoners convicted of low-level crimes and crack cocaine charges, I give credit to him and the bipartisan support within Congress for this. I still think more should be done to address this problem, but this is a start.

Another thing that has more than puzzled me for a long time are the totally unfair trade deals that have been made on behalf of America. China has taken advantage of America for a long time through unfair trade deals, while flooding this country with inferior products. This has enabled them to dump billions of dollars into America, while amassing enormous amounts of real estate and other riches throughout the country. It's amazing that this could have taken place for so long, with the assistance of so many of our elected officials, seemingly in agreement with this lopsided deal.

One thing that I learned early in life concerning business and corruption is to follow the money. But I do understand that the main reason for these absurd trade deals that have broken the backs of hard-working American people is greed. In actuality, the fact that China refused to help Donald Trump along with his reelection bid by helping him strike a compromise to save face is the real reason that he took a stand on unfair trade deals. The best interest of the American people had nothing to do with him making a decision that would be good for this country. By the way, the release of the prisoners was totally political, so the fact remains that he has never done any good for anyone without an ulterior motive.

UNFORGETTABLE LESSON

As a young man, had I understood the true value of math I probably would have studied much harder than I did. But because of my disinterest, my years of not understanding the true value of multiplication and division caused me to be a mathematical late bloomer. In my eighth-grade class at Scullin School in St. Louis, Missouri, I was blessed to have one of the greatest and most effective teachers that I would ever have the pleasure to know, and her name was Billie Mayo.

The mere fact that I have the confidence to write this book today is a direct result of her patience and belief in me. She recognized a talent in me that I didn't see in myself despite my own opposition. Because of her I won a savings bond for writing an essay, **What Americanism Means to Me**. The beauty of that win was more about the pride and confidence it gave me than the actual value of the bond. I could have given the prize away, but the pride—I would have fought tooth and nail for that.

As much as this victory meant to me, there was another impactful lesson that I learned from her and that was the significance of unity. I was always big and strong for my age and I took pride in my strength. She knew this, so she called me up to the front of the class and directed me to hold my hand up and spread my fingers. After spreading them, she directed me to use all my power to prevent her from bending my finger down.

Of course, she bent my finger with ease, with no problem whatsoever. She then called the smallest girl in the class up to the front and directed her to hold up her hand and make a fist. After the little girl made the fist, Mrs. Mayo tried to bend her fingers, to no avail. She then told me, "Fred don't feel bad, it's not your fault. Your separated fingers didn't have a chance when standing alone."

After uplifting me, she then spoke directly to the class with a penetrating message, "Together you are strong, but divided you become weak." Those were some of the most powerful and truthful words that have ever been spoken to me. If a child can understand this, why is it that so many men and women continue to miss the lesson of unity? We remain divided and fighting against one another as if this is the key to life.

AHMAUD ARBERY COULDN'T JOG AND LIVE

On February 23, 2020, another act of hate and racial divide claimed the life of another promising young man, whose only crime was jogging down the street while Black in the state of Georgia. As vicious and shameful as this act of cowardice was toward Ahmaud Arbery, the malicious and unlawful way the local police of Glynn County, Georgia, handled this case was just as horrifying.

The local police allowed the killers to remain free for more than two months after committing this horrific crime without an investigation. The killers, Gregory McMichael and his son, Travis McMichael, told the police that the victim tried to commit a burglary that they hadn't observed, but they wanted to make a citizen's arrest. Their actions led to the death of the young 25-year-old Arbery.

Arbery's family, friends and supporters never accepted the lie the McMichaels told, nor the lawless response of the police. They protested relentlessly for more than two months until finally, a break came in the case. A video showed how the McMichaels followed the jogging Ahmaud Arbery in their pickup truck, stopped him and shot him down in the middle of the street for no apparent reason other than hate.

Even after the emergence of a graphic video showing the senseless and vicious murder, the police and two different district attorneys *still* refused to issue a warrant for their arrest. Finally, after unrelenting national protests, the State of Georgia finally stepped in and arrested these killers.

The arrest of these men is only the beginning of justice and not the end. If this tragedy does not lead to a conviction with a sentence to fit the crime, this will only prove to be another slap in the face for African Americans seeking justice, just like so many times before.

WE ALREADY HAVE THE ROAD MAP FOR EQUALITY AND JUSTICE, LET'S USE IT

We've seen this same story repeatedly with the same results and we continue to hope and pray that justice will prevail. At what point will we come to the realization that this is not working and devise a more organized and impactful strategy to combat the gross injustice that has been perpetrated against us for the ages? I don't claim to have the complete solution for this ongoing travesty, but I do have an idea that I will share.

We must first be honest with ourselves and admit that we are a people that get no respect, not even from one another. This must stop if we **ever** hope to be treated fairly in our own neighborhoods, our country and as we travel the world. We must create POWER AND WEALTH, and this can be done only through the unification of all people of color and those allies that choose to help us advocate for equality

Dr. Martin Luther King, John Lewis, and so many others were truly heroic in their thirst for our civil and human rights while being beaten, flogged and attacked by dogs while protesting in the streets of the country that we helped build. Those protests definitely served their purpose in the '60s, but the boycotts showed us that we must hit the powers that be in their pockets. Anything else will only serve to disrupt the order of things momentarily, without any lasting effect.

This is a totally different time now. There's no need for us to be dragged to jail, beaten in the streets, humiliated and totally disrespected in this day and age. Social media gives us the ability to connect with millions of people instantly and to share more than frivolous activities that only cause more confusion in our lives. These vehicles could easily be used to unite us in a boycott that would truly make a difference today, tomorrow and for the future. This economy could not stand, Wall Street would collapse, and the world would recognize that the masses are a force to be reckoned with.

How could we do this? If we stop spending our money for an agreed period of time, we could assert our true value to the economy. When and for how long would need to be worked out, but the concept is simple. The combined buying power of Black people in this country was around $4 trillion dollars in 2018 and growing. This information that I give is not a secret. It is common knowledge amongst those that care to know. Information alone serves no purpose unless we're prepared to use it.

Let me remind you that the bus boycott that Rev. Dr. Martin Luther King Jr. and others orchestrated was instrumental in the Civil Rights Movement. It is not necessary for us to reinvent the wheel, only improve it by using today's technology, brilliance, and the courage of our young people who are ready to rise and fight for a better world. What are we waiting for? Do we need more Travyon Martins, Eric Garners, Rodney Kings, Sandra Blands, and Michael Browns, not to mention those who weren't caught on video. The time is now!

The proposal of action that I recommended would surely make a difference in the balance of wealth and power, and the magnificent part is, the wealthy would not lose a dime. As a matter of fact, a more equitable world would create more wealth for all because there would be more money circulating in the economy from more people. Over time this would also reduce the rate of poverty, mental illness due to stress and the crime rate would be reduced considerably. Most crimes are not committed by those in the work force, but by the downtrodden, jobless and those that have lost hope.

It sure would be nice to be able to enjoy our neighborhoods without the constant threat of life-endangering criminal activity. But to achieve this we must get out of our comfort zone momentarily in order to bring this dream to fruition. Some of us may never see the fruits of our sacrifices, but our children, grandchildren and generations to come will enjoy the much more peaceful world that we leave them. I'm sure they will forever be thankful to us, for the fearless sacrifices that we make today, on behalf of their precious tomorrow.

KEY ELEMENTS NEEDED FOR OUR OWN WEALTH AND POWER

Now that we've established that wealth and power are essential in the world to operate with any level of fair play and respect, I must now list a few of the most vital components necessary to achieve these goals of prosperity, self-love, pride and empowerment. A plant is only as healthy as its roots, and a building no stronger than its foundation. That's why we must first understand that the makings of a great nation begin within the family. From that root we grow communities, cities, and states that function. From these humble beginnings, a nation is born.

Banks are instrumental for growth and financial power in all communities. This is why we must expand the number of minority-owned banks throughout the country and support these establishments just as passionately as we have supported the likes of Bank of America, U.S. Bank, Chase, and Capital One. These institutions have taken our money for years and treated us like second class citizens. Banks have a critical role in the growth of our economy by lending to credit-worthy borrowers for the purpose of starting businesses, procuring supplies, purchasing equipment and expanding the work force. Healthy banking relationships allow communities to develop their job creators and spur all kinds of positive economic investment, from home ownership to higher education.

When those positive banking relationships are absent, the dreams of minority communities just linger and wither on the vine. Malicious and unfair lending practices from major banks deemed too big to fail allowed our tax dollars to rescue the banking industry that has long refused to rescue us. Truth is, these banks can never fail if they continue to garner our tax dollars and our undying support without offering us any real support in return. Our money only enhances and develops other communities, while our neighborhoods are starved of the capital they need to grow.

EDUCATION IS A MUST

Education is the key to all prosperity. Without a path to a world-class education, the ambitions we have for our next generations are just wishful thinking. I understand that some of our own fathers and mothers and ancestors were denied a formal education and they defied the odds. But their sacrifice and accomplishments served a purpose. They gave us the opportunity to stand on their shoulders and reach for more. They ran the good race, and it's up to each succeeding generation to take the baton and see how far they can run.

As family institutions, we don't want to see our next generation handing off the baton in the same exact spot as the generation before. In fact, we want them to reach goals that we never expected or imagined. Any pursuit other than this would be parental malpractice, a gross and grave disappointment, and a drain on the power and wealth within our communities.

Make no mistake about it, African Americans have contributed some of the most prolific and renowned writers and educators this world has ever known. The first African American owned and operated college in the United States of America was Wilberforce University, which was founded in 1856 near Xenia, Ohio, as a joint venture between the African Methodist Episcopal Church and the Methodist Episcopal Church. This college was named after the eighteenth-century abolitionist William Wilberforce, who was a prominent British philanthropist who pushed to abolish slavery in the US. The introduction of this University played a vital role in reconstruction in the transition from slavery to freedom.

Wilberforce University may have been the first, but many other African American Universities were founded by some of our great men and women who had visions of a better day and brighter future through education. This includes Tuskegee Institute, which was founded in 1881 by Booker T. Washington for the purpose of training African Americans in agriculture and industry to promote the economic progress of his people. Booker T. Washington may be recognized as the founding father of Tuskegee Institute, but the road was paved through the hard work, unselfishness and the inspiration of another man, Lewis Adams. Adams, a former slave, was living a productive life as a tinsmith, harness maker, shoemaker and community leader. Adams was approached by Alabama State Senator W. F. Foster, soon running for reelection, with yet another job offer. The senator offered to pay Lewis to help him gain the support of the African American community in an upcoming election in Macon County, Alabama.

    Instead of accepting the offer of financial gain for his support, Adams requested the senator help him create an educational institution for his people. Adams in his selflessness, even though he had no formal education, saw an opportunity to contribute to the betterment of his people, and Tuskegee Institute was born. Yes, W. F. Foster was re-elected, and the senator kept his promise.

This serves as one of thousands of great stories of the ingenuity and sacrifice our forefathers wielded without any fanfare to help us realize a better future. That list of dedicated people and institutions goes on and on. Hampton University, Fisk University, Morehouse College and so many other schools of higher learning helped produce some of our greatest leaders. At last count there were 107 historically black colleges and universities (HBCU's) in the US. I only hope that the count of black owned and operated universities rises, along with a greater emphasis on creating a curriculum that is more focused on our past, present and future greatness.

Education is key to the development of *all* communities, as it promotes economic and social advancement and gives us all a better understanding of what it takes to elevate our communities and ourselves. Education gives us hope and pride, along with the ability to communicate and share our information and talent with the greater world.

THERE'S NO CONNECTION WITHOUT COMMUNICATION

Communication also enhances our ability to connect with people of other cultures and nationalities as well as within our own families and communities. Communication breakdowns are a key source of dysfunction along the whole spectrum, from families to nations. Through communication comes trust, understanding and even empathy for others. It is plain to see that so many of us demonstrate a lack of communication skills every day.

Everyone wants their plight understood, but no one cares to listen half as much as they care to be understood. This epidemic of deafness allows us to walk around covering our ears to the other guy's complaints, oblivious to any cries for help but our own. That's likely our instinct as human beings. Add to that tendency many well-executed and well-financed campaigns to further that divisiveness for the benefit of those who stand to gain. We're all listening to our own song of woe, covering our ears to each other's complaints in a dysfunctional competition for help or attention. Meanwhile the wealthy ignore us all and dance away to a completely different tune.

THE IMPORTANCE OF VALUES

The economy is important for the growth and well-being of communities, but there are other components that are just as important to fragile neighborhoods. For decades, shared values have held poor black communities together in the absence of wealth. So many have forgotten and disregarded the principles that made our neighborhoods rich in spirit if not in coin. Our children knew their value to the community. They didn't devalue themselves so easily for things.

This is why we must have leaders in all capacities that are equipped with strong values; who will remember and honor their constituents back home; whose actions will not differ in the dark of night, as opposed to the light of day. We must have politicians that are motivated to head to Washington with a mission to get things done back home on the block. I know that may seem impossible in this corrupt world that we live in, but when we hold folks accountable for their actions, they can provide the nudge needed to keep everyone's eyes on the prize.

The absence of values in leadership and incompetence, has most certainly cast a giant shadow over the dwindling hope among America's middle class. Outside of the extraordinarily wealthy, most Americans are in a state of darkness in America right now. Donald Trump has proved himself to be totally absent of any moral compass, and his Republican cronies seem to have adopted his DNA, which only serves to further depress hope among poor people and people of color in this country.

I prefer to think of myself as an eternal optimist, which is in *my* DNA. Our forefathers and mothers struggled for centuries through horrifying conditions while still passing on values of peace, human dignity, human rights and freedom. These values are the guiding principles that keeps my hope from ever being dampened or suppressed.

As a matter of fact, I believe this recent spate of modern-day lynchings and the brazen lawlessness with which they've occurred will only serve as a beacon of light in the end. We've been asleep, lulled into a false state of comfortability with our second-class citizenship. Now we can confront the fact that these injustices won't stop unless we stop them. These people who continue to impose their will on us, have no values that will ever result in any fair play for the common folks, only for the rich and entitled.

Former President Barrack Obama's address to the graduating class of 2020 was right on point when he said,

> *"More than anything, this pandemic has fully, finally torn back the curtain on the idea that so many of the folks in charge don't know what they're doing. A lot of them aren't even pretending to be in charge. If the world's going to be better, it's going to be up to you."*

Former President Obama's outstanding contribution to the world's economic recovery can't be appreciated enough. I, for one, couldn't have been prouder of his accomplishments in office. Not only that, he and his wife, the former first lady, Michelle Obama, always displayed exemplary morals and integrity. But his greatest accomplishment, I believe, may have come totally without his intention. Because of him, we have fully unmasked the unvarnished hatred for people of color that still exists in this country.

THE POWER OF PAIN AND FEAR

The racist, confused people committing so many random acts of violence are only further emboldened by the constant stream of inflammatory statements from our leaders. Our president's fearmongering followed by his low-key reassurance to these people that they will not be held accountable for their actions puts all kinds of people in a dangerous situation. Fear is a profoundly motivating tactic, for good or for bad.

Pain and fear, arguably the two most powerful motivators, are followed quickly by greed, which is quickly closing in for first place in the halls of Congress. When used right, fear can be the motivating force that brings about accountability and some sense of fair play. But when used with evil intent, it only deepens the divide between Americans who should be willing to see and aid one another. Let's not fall for the misdirect. Why continue to dampen our own hopes of happiness, prosperity and a brighter future in a world that has so much to offer?

No community or country will ever realize its greatness as long as so many people continue to live in fear and under oppression. This country was built in part through the pain, fear and loss of its early inhabitants, some simply because they were the wrong hue. That doesn't sound like a civilized country, at least not for everyone.

RESPECT

There are so many components that make up the ingredients of a healthy and ambitious society, but I choose to list respect as the final ingredient for our purposes here. Respect will help us build the more fair and prosperous country we all want to live in.

Real respect is when you can accept and appreciate others, even if you don't agree with their ideals or feelings. It is only necessary to have an appreciation for them and what they believe in to understand their underlying importance. Respect builds not only trust and admiration; it allows you to empathize with those that have different experiences than you have had.

True respect is not forced through intimidation, fear or oppression, but earned through one's deeds and actions. When you are in a seat of power that gives you the ability to impose your will on others, you have a part to play in guiding your people to a higher place.

MY DRUG USE

For more than twenty years I was engaged in the everyday use of illegal drugs, preferably heroin and sometimes cocaine. I found myself in a constant state of lawlessness which included a total lack of respect for the property or life of others. Through my many years of drug use, I very seldom worked a job, therefore I became a hustler who traveled all over the country, finding different ways to get money for the sole purpose of feeding my drug habit.

Through one of my many travels I found myself in Pittsburg, Pennsylvania, with two partners of mine, Red and George, two of the best till tappers to ever come out of the city of St. Louis. Till tappers generally work in a team of two or three, in stores or other businesses. If the team is working correctly, someone will distract while the other takes money from the cash register or safe.

Things went well for us once we started our travel going east from St. Louis. We made money and got high at our leisure, but once we got to Pittsburg, our luck broke bad. Red got locked up trying to go over a six-foot-high plexiglass barrier to take some money. He was caught on the spot. George called home and had money for a plane ticket sent to him. That left me all alone, which was okay, but soon thereafter, my car broke down and all the money I made was gone.

At least my car broke down on a street in a residential neighborhood and I didn't have to worry about it getting towed right away. Not only that, but I was close to Center and Wiley streets, which is where the drugs were. I could have called home also, but my pride wouldn't allow that. I considered myself *"staying tough and staying true to the game."*

I slept in the car and every morning I would walk to Center and Wiley street so that I could get a ride to go hustling in order to get more drugs. I never got enough money to fix my car. It was bad. I'd never been at a place this low in my life. When I wasn't locked up, I was tired and frustrated with a drug habit that was way out of control. I couldn't see a way out.

This routine of sleeping in my car had been going on for almost a week. I'll never forget that final Sunday morning in the car. I was sleep, and out of nowhere I heard a knock on the car window that startled me. I looked up, but I couldn't see a face, only an image that I didn't recognize. Soon there came a man's voice that simply asked, *"Are you hungry?"*

"Yes," I said,

"Do you want to come eat breakfast with me and my family?"

"Yes,"

"Well come on in," he said, while pointing to a house directly across the street.

He quickly disappeared, going through the door of the house that he had pointed to. After getting myself into a more conscious state of mind, I walked over to the house and knocked on the door, not really knowing what to expect. I hadn't met many decent people recently, only thugs and cutthroats. All of a sudden, the door flew open and there stood a man about six feet tall with that same familiar voice that I heard in the car.

"Come on in my brother," he said, while extending his hand as if to escort me into his home. "Follow me to the bathroom so that you can clean yourself up."

I did just that. He handed me a washcloth and closed the door behind himself. I washed up good, as quick as possible. I then exited the bathroom and there he stood.

"Follow me," he said. Upon entering the room I followed him to, I was pleased to see his family.

"Have a seat right here."

I took a seat while he began to introduce himself and his family to me, and I introduced myself to them. This setting reminded me of an old hometown breakfast with family and loved ones. With him were his wife and two kids, a girl and a boy, both looking to be about ten or eleven years of age, and his mother. She was beautiful, having a look of warmth and concern. I couldn't believe my eyes at the sight of all the food on the table: chicken, potatoes smothered with gravy, eggs, pancakes and so much more. I couldn't see how the table could hold all this food. I was soon interrupted from my gaze with his words.

"Let us all hold hands in prayer," the head

of the household said. After blessing the food, they all seemed to cater to me.

"Just let me know what you want, and don't be bashful," his wife said, "We want you to get good and full."

She fixed my plate, and we all ate as if I was one of the family. It was all just so unbelievable to have someone take me into their home, if only for a moment, and show me so much kindness and concern. There was no pity, but a true sense of their appreciation for me as a person through the conversation we had as we ate. I was more than happy to open up to them about my life, without going too far, and the more we talked the more intrigued they seemed to become and the more they wanted to talk to me. It was if they didn't want me to leave, but I knew that I would soon give them my thanks of appreciation.

Before I could get my thoughts together, the man looked me straight in the eye and asked, "How did you get here, it just don't make sense."

"What do you mean." I asked, knowing all the time what he was talking about.

"After talking to you I don't understand how you could be in the position that you're in, it seems to me that you could be a success in anything that you chose to do."

"Bad decisions," I answered in a low embarrassed voice, while they all stared at me in awe, as if waiting on me to further elaborate on my answer. But there was nothing else to say. It didn't make sense to me, either, but I couldn't explain to them that I was caught up in a whirlwind that I didn't know how to exit, I just had to ride it out.

We all said our goodbyes and well wishes, but before I could leave, his mother handed me a big brown bag.

"There's plenty of food in there, I don't want you to be hungry," she said, while at the same time slipping a twenty-dollar bill into my hand. She then held my hand and said, "God bless you, and don't you ever sit out there in that car hungry, just knock on the door."

"Thanks again," I said as I walked away, still not believing the act of kindness and respect that had just been bestowed on me. I didn't feel worthy, and I knew that I was on my way to spend that twenty on some drugs. I felt like I was betraying those good people, but I realized that I was powerless, as I begin my walk to Center and Wiley. Those good people could have easily called the police and had me removed, but they chose to not be afraid and at the same time, show me respect when I certainly hadn't earned it. For the life of me I can't remember the name of that most gracious family, but I do know that I will never forget what they did to help me turn my life around.

I share this story to give all readers a better view of my journey, so that who I am today can be better understood. This moment in my life was fuel for the engine that began my resurrection for the sake of myself, and for many families to come, not just my own.

THE KNEE ON GEORGE FLOYD'S NECK

"I can't breathe, I can't breathe!"

No, this is not Eric Garner this time. These are now the last words cried out by George Floyd, a black man killed by four White police officers in broad daylight in the city of Minneapolis, Minnesota. Not only was this tragedy executed in the light of day, but it was done in the presence of several on-lookers begging the police not to kill him.

They shouted out repeatedly *"He's dying, he's bleeding from his nose,"* while one of the policemen continued to press his knee into Floyd's neck, as he lay on the ground, handcuffed. This public lynching took place while two other officers put their knees on his back and a fourth stood by watching, trying to quiet the crowd instead of stopping this obvious murder. The only difference between this public police execution and so many in the past is that all four officers were fired immediately instead of the usual rehearsed phrases, assuring the public that an investigation will be performed.

This is still miles apart from what true justice demands, because these killers should have been arrested immediately after the viewing of the video, just as anyone else would have been if they didn't have the protection of the badge or mere white privilege. Either of those two possessions are sufficient cover when it comes to taking Black lives.

POLICE KILL BREONNA TAYLOR WHILE SHE SLEEPS

I had started another chapter of this book, but the killing of George Floyd was so horrific that it was imperative that I shine more light on these latest flagrant injustices that now seem to be an everyday occurrence here in the United States of America. I only hope that at some point the daily executions and grave injustices visited on Black people will stop long enough for me to share my views on some other topics. It won't be easy, now that I think about it, because I haven't even mentioned the home invasion and killing of an emergency medical worker, 26-year-old Breonna Taylor in Louisville, Kentucky.

Without knocking or announcing themselves, the police burst through the door of Taylor's apartment while she slept with her gentleman friend, Kenneth Walker. Walker shot back at the police, not knowing who they were. He only knew that he was being attacked in his home by an unknown intruder.

This is the account of the story that was

given by Walker's attorney, along with the admission by police that the man that they were looking for was already in jail. Each and everybody camera that these police wore were all conveniently turned off throughout this raid. I must also mention that the gun that Walker had was registered, and he was allowed by law to have this weapon. Walker was arrested immediately and was being held in jail for a charge of attempted murder, while these killers of his lady, Breonna Taylor, remained free and on the police payroll.

There was more than one tragedy for this family on this night, according to Breonna Taylor's mother, Tamika Palmer. After finding out about a disturbance at her daughter's apartment, Palmer went straight there like any loving parent would, to find her child. Upon arrival, she was told by the police posted outside Breonna's apartment that Breonna had been taken to the hospital by an ambulance. So she left immediately, headed for the hospital seeking answers about Breonna.

After reaching the hospital in record time, she was then told by the charge nurse to go to the waiting room and was promised that someone would get back with her as soon as they had information about her daughter. After waiting for over two hours without hearing anything back from the nurse, Ms. Palmer went back to the desk only to find a different nurse. She asked this nurse about Breonna, and to her dismay, she knew nothing about this situation, nor did she know that Palmer had been in the waiting room.

The new nurse then told Ms. Palmer to wait at the desk and to give her a few minutes to get some information about her daughter. After returning, the nurse informed her that there was no Breonna Taylor anywhere in the hospital, and she wasn't on her way to the hospital either. *"This is unbelievable!"* she thought, but there was no time to express her anger, she had to get back to Breonna's apartment immediately.

Her sense of urgency was increasing every moment, while she continued to fight off any feelings of dread. When she pulled up to the apartment there were only a few police officers standing outside now, but they informed her that she couldn't enter the apartment because there was still an investigation taking place. She then asked an officer to let her know something about Breonna.

"Okay, I'll check right away." he told her, and he quickly entered the apartment—but he never came out. Several hours passed, until finally a different officer came out.

"Where is my daughter, where is Breonna?" she shouted.

"She's in the house," the officer told her. At that moment she felt like she had been hit with a gut punch that took all the wind out of her body, and she knew her baby was gone.

Her greatest fear was proven to be true. Breonna had lain dead in the apartment all night while the police gave her bad information that only caused this nightmare of a moment to drag on all night. What a horrible way to treat a mother at a time like this. The question is, why did they stall all night? It was not an accident; I can assure you of that. They were already viewing Ms. Palmer across that great divide that made her less a citizen to be protected and served, and more a problem to be handled. It takes a total lack of empathy or respect of Black people in this country to dishonor the dead with no regard for the families. We see this repeatedly. This has to stop. I remind you all that a **NATION-WIDE BOYCOTT** is the answer to the start of sincere changes that must take place in this country—*immediately*. This needs to be done in conjunction with protesting and all other means of applying relentless pressure to big business and the establishment.

THE PROTEST

O say can you see,
by the dawn's early light,
what so proudly we hailed
at the twilight's last gleaming...
Of the march and protesting that erupted into
fights.

No this is not the War of 1812 when a Maryland Fort was bombarded by the British from whence the Star-Spangled Banner derived. This is the protest of 2020 right here, in these United States of America. Burnt buildings, houses destroyed, and multiple protesters hurt, arrested and totally exhausted from a long night of fighting for the freedom and safety that has been denied people of color for far too long. Police officers and protestors throughout this country and other countries all around the world, have been injured or died, and my fear is that we have a long way to go before it ends.

These protests were originally ignited because of the public lynching of George Floyd and his infamous, familiar cry, *"I can't breathe."* Just like the cries of Eric Garner, whose killers suffered no accountability. The policeman in that case actually choked him to death and only lost his job six years after his death. What a shame! And now our officials have the nerve to look us in the eye and ask for patience in order to allow the legal process to work.

Don't get it twisted for one minute, these two killings are not the only murders that have added fuel to the anger that now burns in the streets. These acts of total disregard, the taking of so many lives by police all over the country is nothing new for us. This has been happening forever. This violence coupled with centuries of systemic oppression, depression, joblessness and unfair treatment continues to haunt us no matter how much progress we try to make.

All of these disparities coupled with the state of cabin fever setting in due to the coronavirus, has created a ripeness for prolonged protests. All over the world for a week now, every day new protests have continued, through days of peaceful marching and nights of fighting, shooting, looting and the burning of buildings in cities all over the country.

CHAPTER II: GLOBAL DIVIDE

A GLOBAL DIVIDE HAS WORSENED THIS PANDEMIC

A global divide between haves and have nots has a lot to do with why we find ourselves so deep in the jaws of this pandemic. The coronavirus is exposing countries to their core, while leaving so many leaders befuddled and lost.

As sovereign nations each try to respond to the needs of their people and guide them through this pandemic, the strong men of the world are leading their nations on a path of destruction. I believe at some point we will get past this beast of a virus responsible for Covid-19, but because of our own arrogance and continued selfishness it will take much longer than is necessary.

Could this coronavirus be the latest in a series of attempts at a genocide of the poor, oppressed and disenfranchised people of the world? Could this virus have arrived just in time to be a convenient foil to help the power elite hold on to a power base that is eroding and growing younger and more diverse by the minute? I don't like igniting conspiracy theories, but I also wouldn't underestimate the evil depths by which people in power seek to maintain it. To slow-walk a response to a novel coronavirus decimating poor people of color is in keeping with historical norms. It wouldn't be the first time human beings were scapegoated and targeted for a slow death, and it likely wouldn't be the last. As outrageous as this may sound, no one ever went to trial for the fate of indigenous people. Free land "discovered" and "settled"—that's how the story went down. Our language has sanitized the hate crimes right out of history.

Those impacted most by crises are always poor people. Those farther up the economic ladder may fare better, but don't think the destruction won't reach the so-called middle class – you are ***not*** excluded. And neither are the millions of people living in poverty in these underdeveloped countries all over the world, whose deaths are not even being calculated. We're not being tested at the rate deemed necessary by the doctors and scientists in America. Do you think for one minute that those people in all of these poor countries are getting tested? Not so, and once we think that we have a hold on this beast in our developed nations, the virus from these underdeveloped communities will reach out and grab civilization again.

All countries that waddle in enormous riches must realize that, regardless of how many walls we erect, our connection to our global family is inseparable. This is why we must share our blessings before catastrophes strike. Our fates are always tied to the least of these.

I'm not pointing a finger at any country in

particular, but what sense does it make for a few people in a few countries to amass more wealth than they could possibly spend for generations, while leaving so many people all over the world in poverty? The neglect we allow will haunt us in one way or another.

Is it in our nature or is it a learned behavior that causes us to continue to be blinded by greed and selfishness? Have we not yet learned that we create our own destruction when we're completely unconcerned with those less fortunate? It would make more sense for wealthy nations of the world to come together for the purpose of uplifting the under resourced people and countries of the world. That would be much cheaper than the enormous amounts we squander on wars. True altruism, and I don't mean invading these places for the purpose of robbing them of their remaining wealth, is the evolved response of advanced nations.

I do understand that there have been several attempts to uplift failing countries that have failed, but global problems deserve a global response. All countries must attack this problem collectively, with money and resources. Of course, you can't just pump money into a country and expect corruption not to rear its ugly head. This has failed before and this method will continue to fail if we don't reinvent our methods.

All nations have a part to play in the stabilization of developing countries. Shared wealth is necessary if we ever hope to have any semblance of global reform.

Just as within a family, global family members may drift apart, but the fighting can only go so far. If any family member experiences problems too enormous to be handled alone, extended family show up to lend a hand. Altruism may sound naïve, but it has a way of benefitting all involved in the end. I hope that during this health crises countries will be more than willing to work together and recognize it's in our global best interest to help one another. But we wealth holders have become so wrapped up in "me" and "I" that it has become practically impossible to get past ourselves, even in a time of crisis.

Crises have a profound impact on our mental health and future. This current crisis reminds me of a time when I was a child in the late 1950s. The houses on 4th Street near where we lived in St. Louis, Missouri, flooded, but families didn't have to struggle through their loss alone. Neighbors from near and far joined in to help without any hesitation or any consideration of past differences.

I saw men, women and some children, too, using buckets to dump water out of the houses while others stacked sandbags in front of the houses to prevent more water from getting in.

As a child this was amazing to me, to see so many people working together in total harmony, whose only reward was the satisfaction of helping a neighbor in need. I'm sure many people can relate to losing everything in a flood. We've all played the good neighbor or been the neighbor in need at some time.

The sheer magnitude of this COVID-19 crisis far outweighs anything I've experienced in my lifetime. We should all call upon our better angels and remember instances when others showed up for us. We should let those recollections serve as blueprints for how to move forward in a post-COVID-19 world. It all seems insurmountable now, but through small acts of kindness and consideration, we will survive.

The secret ingredient to surviving this crisis **is** unity, as just displayed in the world-wide protests that took place for George Floyd and black and brown people all over the world. This tragedy could not be contained in Minneapolis, Minnesota nor is America big enough to hold this monstrous injustice, because this miscarriage of justice is not limited to any one country or continent. It has proved to be a disease that has only become more vicious and sophisticated as time goes by. This art of oppression and the continued ability of the powers that be to keep their knee on our necks crosses borders. Shared information and solidarity have to be some of the world's most valuable commodities. It always has been. Only now information technologies allow us to organize and share our plans more easily than ever before.

Not Perfectly Divided

As large a role as information technology has played in dividing the masses, new technologies could very well backfire on those in power. New types of media are uniting the oppressed all over the world. Thanks to tech savvy organizers, organic protests sprang up in the UK, France, Brazil, Australia, all over Latin America, Asia, Africa and elsewhere in support of the Black Lives Matter movement inspired by the death of George Floyd. The time is ripe for the strong but less affluent to inherit their just due.

Just imagine young people the world over discovering their power, connecting with millions of people all over the globe at a moment's notice to share in a common goal. The power of their joint protests and influence is almost unimaginable.

I thought I had a good understanding of what was happening with this movement, but I was in for quite a surprise. I've been in marches before, but on June 1, 2020, I marched in St. Louis as we shut down Highway 40, and I must admit that the feeling of appreciation, strength and the pride that welled up and through me was so fulfilling! Just to witness thousands of our young freedom fighters, putting their all on the line for a better day. Unafraid, relentless and so conscious of what we've been through and where we're headed. This march, unlike anything that I've ever witnessed, was loaded with all nationalities from all parts of the world and filled with love, joy and purpose.

Once I talked to other protestors, I realized that they appreciated me just as much as I appreciated them, and yes, we were all in this together.

After the march I was floating on the wings of pride and hope, not realizing that I would soon get another jolt that would propel me to even greater heights. That's right, once I returned home and turned on the news, I then realized that there were marches and protests by so many young freedom fighters *all over the world*. Our young people in the United States took to the streets in an open invitation to join a struggle that was of worldwide interest, and the world responded.

The fire, wit and determination of our youth is inspiring. It's the same type of fire that made Dr. Martin Luther King Jr., at the age of twenty-six, become the leader of a new Civil Rights movement. He worked along with other young freedom fighters such as his wife, Coretta Scott King, Bayard Rustin, who helped organize the Montgomery Bus Boycott, Rosa Parks, James Farmer, the leader of the Congress of Racial Equality (CORE) and a follower of Mahatma Gandhi's non-violent movement, and Hosea Williams, who assisted with black voter registration. Their youth and fire are what propelled them to progress. This ingenuity and determination are what I see now in so many of our youth today. They are ready and willing to take the baton. They will succeed too if we only give them our support along the way.

I don't think it's an accident that talent materializes to meet historic moments. At the dawn of this new Civil Rights movement, an amazing surge in youth leadership finds us well prepared for the challenges ahead.

These young leaders today have found a way to unite across nationalities to form a real rainbow coalition. This summer's protests may prove to be as significant as Muhammad Ali's stand against the war in Vietnam or Colin Kaepernick's taking of the knee during the national anthem.

Let's not ever forget the determination of Nelson Mandela, who, through his own choice, submitted to imprisonment in South Africa for twenty-seven years in his fight against apartheid. This system of institutionalized racial segregation maintained a hold on South Africa and South West Africa from 1948 until April 27, 1994, with the formation of a democratic government.

An offer of freedom was made to Nelson Mandela several times during his twenty-seven-year incarceration with one condition; that he end his war against apartheid. But due to his relentless pursuit of **real** freedom for himself and the people of South Africa, he repeatedly turned down those insulting offers. Years of unjustified incarceration in the hell-like conditions of some of the most notorious prisons in South Africa followed. Not only did he survive these devastating conditions while incarcerated, but he gained his freedom with his morals and integrity intact, armed with plans to dismantle this unjust government and the ideology of apartheid.

Mandela understood that his release didn't result from his government's sudden desire to right its wrong. Instead, Mandela's influence was needed to calm the tidal wave of domestic and international pressure and the threat of a racial civil war. F. W. de Klerk, who was president at the time, ordered Mandela's release with the assurance that there would be serious negotiations for free and democratic elections. As a result of this election the African National Congress, which was led by Nelson Mandela, won the election. He was inaugurated on May 10, 1994 as the first Black president and he then named F. W. de Klerk as his Deputy President.

Great changes can never be accomplished through small sacrifices. Muhammad Ali never envisioned losing years of his career and being persecuted by the government and most White people because of his refusal to fight a war that he didn't believe in. Nelson Mandela didn't plan to sacrifice twenty-seven years of his life in degrading conditions when he dreamt of a way to overthrow apartheid. But he endured and, as a result of his endurance, he maintained power with his people, he gained freedom, his dream of ending apartheid was realized and he became president of the same country that had once treated him so cruelly.

Dr. Martin Luther King Jr. knowingly gave his life in the struggle for our civil and human rights and he told us so in his last speech.

"Somewhere I read of the freedom of assembly. Somewhere I read of the freedom of speech. Somewhere I read of the freedom of press. Somewhere I read that the greatness of America is the right to protest for rights.

"And so, just as I said, we aren't going to let dogs or water hoses turn us around. We aren't going to let any injunction turn us around. We are going on. Go out and tell your neighbors not to buy **Coca-Cola** in Memphis. Go and tell them not to buy **Sealtest** milk. Tell them not to buy what is the other bread? **Wonder Bread**. And what is the other bread company Jesse? Tell them not to buy **Hart's Bread**.

"As Jesse Jackson has said, up to now, only the garbage men have been feeling the pain; now we must kind of redistribute the pain. Well, I don't know what will happen now. We've got some difficult days ahead. But it really doesn't matter with me now, because I've been to the mountaintop. And I don't mind.

Like anybody, I would like to live a long life; longevity has its place. But I'm not concerned about that now. I just want to do God's Will. And He's allowed me to go to the mountain. And I've looked over. And I've seen the Promised Land. I may not get there with you. But I want you to know tonight, that we, as a people, will get to the Promised Land. So, I'm happy, tonight. I'm not worried about anything. I'm not fearing any man. '*Mine Eyes have seen the glory of the coming of the Lord.*'"

These words along, with his actions that followed, shows the surety of his understanding that his life would not last long if the fight continued, yet fight on he did.

We may never have heard the famous portion of the **I Have a Dream** speech without the urging of the great sister, Mahaila Jackson saying, "*Tell them about the dream Martin, tell them about the dream*". After her request, Martin regrouped, contemplated, and began to deliver the thunderous message we're all so familiar with.

You'll note that Dr. King called for protests, but he knew boycotts were also needed because individually Black people were poor, but together they were an economic powerhouse that would be hard to ignore. And, if companies didn't respond to the demands of this unified effort, they could not stand and would soon be out of business.

The magnificent movement led by Dr. Martin Luther King Jr. was not the only movement that displayed true grit in that era. The Honorable Elijah Muhammad, through his wisdom and superior organizational skills, worked to instill pride in a people that had only known self-depreciation and a lack of self-worth. He understood that unmasking the truth about Europeans was necessary, in order to enable his people to have the courage to grow, gain their independence, and learn to stop relying on the acceptance of the dominant culture. Through his teachings we were blessed with so many men and women of greatness, whose lives were fully devoted to the cause of Black people.

The Honorable Elijah Muhammad taught economic development. He was instrumental in forming educational institutions that, since their inception, have been owned and operated by and for Black people which has proven to be a huge success and still exists today under the leadership of one of his greatest students, the Honorable Minister Louis Farrakhan.

The Nation of Islam, started by the Master Wallace Fard Muhammad, has Mosques throughout the country under the leadership of Louis Farrakhan, and has even gone abroad to other countries to spread his message of creating Black wealth and power.

The Nation of Islam has ties to many African

Muslims who were enslaved here in the United States throughout the nineteenth century. Their original faith was resurrected in the twentieth century through the teachings of the Prophet Noble Drew Ali, who founded the Moorish Science Temple of America. Wallace Fard Muhammad's association with Nobel Drew led Muhammad to establish the Nation of Islam. This movement from international sources is still active today as a multiracial movement.

The remedy to the oppression that we face is still the same, and the time is now ripe. We can't knock this unjust world structure down with a jab, we must throw combination punches repeatedly with protests, sit-ins, shut outs, and boycotts, along with a well-designed plan to right these wrongs and lift the knee on our necks for now and for the ages.

We must keep in mind that this movement is global, therefore shared information between all nations that are in pursuit of change is mandatory if we choose to go big, instead of piecemeal. Too often our leaders rely solely on their own level of understanding and reject information from other sources that have already been met with success. Although the movement is strong the results will take time, especially on the global stage. America has a new opportunity to be a beacon of light in a world of darkness.

There's a global uprising in effect now, the

likes of which the world has never seen before and may never see again. If the voice of the people is not heard in this moment it may never be heard. We must not allow empty promises nor minor changes to halt this momentum that our young people have created through their harmonious voices, here in America and all over the globe. Hong Kong, China, Australia, Canada, the United Kingdom, New Zealand, the Philippines, Israel, Haifa, even in the city of Bethlehem and so many more, people have stood up to fight for the rights we all so fully deserve. This lopsided balance of wealth and power has had a choke hold on the growth of the world's economy, progress, civil and human rights for ages—but the time for all of that is coming to an end.

MODERN DAY SLAVERY

Slavery is still prominent all over the world, but the people of India, China, Russia, the US, Brazil, Germany and Australia have felt its impact the most. The United States is reported to have hundreds of thousands, of modern-day slaves, but this count is far from accurate because we don't include the millions of prisoners that are forced to work for free. And to make matters worse, so many of these people were imprisoned due to poverty, along with unjust laws, that were put in place for the sole purpose of free labor. Those things coupled with the fact that systemic racism exists globally, has proven to be a major tool in the cause for oppression.

I feel the need to peel a layer off the whole concept of slavery, because in my view, the obvious modern-day parallel are the millions of, people working for subsistence wages, earning minimum wage. That's right, minimum wage is nothing more than slavery on free land. It enables the slave to move to and from destinations that are necessary for them to provide food, shelter and clothing for their families and not much more. It's a shame that our monied populace won't share some of the wealth, and now the healthcare that had been afforded to so many, may soon be stripped away through the viciousness of this ruthless administration. I'm not just talking about minorities, either. This includes anybody that fits in the impoverished category, which includes so many of Trump's supporters. But an adage still holds true today: some people will cut off their nose to spite their face. People! Think about what you're doing to yourselves, not to mention all the other people that are victims just like you are.

There is a big difference between the oppression experienced in most countries and here in America. The difference is, so many people here continue to give permission through their votes to keep their oppressors in office; to assure that their own state of servitude remains intact. This does not hold true in most nations because, for the most part, their way of life is forced on them through a dictatorship or a ruling body that doesn't allow dissent. And to prove my point, there are many occasions that so called "strong men dictators" have turned their military forces on the people and killed off thousands of innocent people for protesting the lawless rule of a mad regime.

In 2011 Bashar al-Assad, Syria's President, gave orders for his military to open fire on innocent, unarmed protestors which resulted in the deaths of more than 2,000 civilians and 400 security forces. In 2011, thousands of demonstrators in Egypt took to Cairo's Tahrir Square calling for an end to the rule of then President Hosni Mubarak, only to be met by gun fire from their own country's military forces that resulted in the death of 850 civilians. These two separate tragedies displayed a level of total disregard for the lives of citizens who only wanted to be a voice for change.

These misguided massacres grew out of an attempt to dominate people already living in an oppressed state. They chose to take a stand against a greater domination. Even though no one died on June 1, 2020 when Donald Trump unleashed military forces on innocent protestors in Lafayette Square directly across the street from the White House, it could have easily escalated out of control, just like the actions we've read about in Syria and Egypt. The only reason this aggression was ordered was so that Donald Trump could have a photo op in front of Ashburton House, the parish house of St. John's Episcopal Church, while holding an upside-down Bible in his hand.

The day prior to this assault, protestors were outside the White House in great numbers. This frightened the president and aroused his autocratic "want to be" strong man tendencies, so he retreated to his White House bunker. This cowardly retreat caused embarrassment on his part, so he lied and said that he only went to the bunker to inspect it, just in case it had to be used in the future. This didn't go over as well as he had hoped, so bunker boy (as some began to call him) decided on the Bible photo op to distract from the idea that he was cowering in fear inside the White House. The nickname fit him like a measured coat.

The sacrifices of so many freedom fighters current, present and future will guide us through this next critical phase. Let's be inspired by the culmination of a long struggle. We can finally grab a hold of our destiny.

Not Perfectly Divided

Fred Easter

CHAPTER III COMMUNITY DIVIDE

    Our communities continue to experience poverty and crime due to long-standing systemic issues while suffering a serious lack of empathy from the outside world. The deeper the divide between our poor neighborhoods of color and the rest of the world, the greater the animosity these communities face for the systemic problems that they cannot solve on their own. In a spiral of suspicion and hatred, poor black and brown people become trapped in neighborhoods that are collapsing economically, socially and spiritually and are then blamed for that very collapse.

    Wealth and social status can insulate us from some of the harshness of life, but it cannot wall us off from the problems of the world. The problem with allowing communities to collapse under their own weight is that we all still must live in the world with the inhabitants of these neighborhoods, and people without hope make poor choices that affect all of us. Whether upper class, upper middle class, middle class, working class or poor, at some point our fates intersect.

    Economically the upper class has made it past subsistence level issues, and can devote their time, education, talent and resources to protecting and maintaining the level of wealth and privilege they've obtained. In this way our fates are self-sustaining, with those already succeeding able to protect their status and sacred fraternities to ensure further success. The upper middle class are deeply invested in two types of movement—the desire for upward mobility and the fear of a downward fall. Since most of our nations' wealth now lies with the families of the one percent, our economic strivers in the middle face more competition for a smaller and smaller piece of the pie.

The middle class in this country are in a precarious position. For the most part living paycheck to paycheck, life in the middle means one missed check could spell disaster. A steep downward spiral is never more than a major illness or pink slip away. In a turn of absolute madness, this vulnerable population has been rescuing the American economy with a thin mirage of upward mobility for literally decades. This spending and striving for a lifestyle that is scarcely attainable keeps our economic engine humming along even though these families have no savings, and no safety net should the worst befall them.

Those living on minimum wage and minimal education would probably be described as the working class. These normally hard working and dedicated family people have learned the art of sacrifice and are masters of delayed gratification. Securing a better future for their family is far more important than their own immediate interests. True heroes are what I prefer to call these people, probably because this is the type of household that I grew up in. Now that I look back on it, it was amazing how my mom and dad stretched the few dollars that came into our household. Simply amazing!

Before my family moved to the north side of St. Louis, we lived on the south side at 2222 Rutger St. This was a very tight knit community, and everyone seemed to know each other. The boundaries of our neighborhood for the kids were very liberal from east to west, but the northern and southern borders were quite different. My parents didn't allow me to go past Chouteau without supervision to the north.

The southern end of Lafayette St. was the cutoff, with only a total of six blocks in between. White people occupied the neighborhoods past there and anytime we went south of Lafayette we would have to fight or run for our lives. Fighting was a way of life, but I found out how fast I could run while being south of Lafayette, and the White boys realized how fast they could run and jump when they got caught *north* of Lafayette St. I can recall once or twice that we came to blows with one another, but no one ever died. However, the fear and hatred remained intact.

I didn't realize until later in life that there was a big difference in having neighbors and living in a community. And, if you've never lived in a community, you would have no way of ever knowing the difference.

As a child, before I was even ten years old, I can remember doing all sorts of mischievous and childish things that I thought I had gotten away with, only to find out when I got home that my parents already knew about my exploits. This is because everyone knew me, and everyone was a part of our family and held me and all the other kids accountable for our bad deeds—and good ones too. In some cases, I would be chastised by the other moms and dads in the neighborhood before I even made it home. And let me make this perfectly clear, I knew not to call any of these people liars! If I had, I may not be alive today to tell this story!

Police officers in our communities can play a significant role in our lives. As much as I oppose the actions of aggressive policing then and now, I know, in spite of the life of lawlessness that I lived for much of my adult life, there are so many good police officers out there, as evidenced by one story from my childhood.

I was about eight or nine years of age when a couple of friends of mine and I decided to play hooky from school with, in our minds, a genius plan on how to fill the time. We put our money together, bought a foot-long poor boy sandwich, divided it equally, got some Vess soda from the Vess Soda Company a few blocks away. We would eat and hide out all over the neighborhood. Well, part of the plan was fulfilled when we got the sandwich and soda and made it to an alley where we begin to eat and drink. But before I could get two good bites of my piece of the sandwich, the local police drove into the alley and jumped out of the car before we could move.

We didn't try to run, but I did have time to let my buddies know to let me do the talking. I just knew that I could explain us out of this foolish situation that we found ourselves in.

"How are you guys doing," The officer asked.

"Just fine sir," I countered.

"Why aren't you all in school?"

"We got excused for the rest of the day,"

"Why?"

"Uhhhhh" my words begin to tremor and run together. I was falling apart, but I quickly recovered, "Because, our teacher got sick and had to go home for the day."

"Do your parents know about this?"

"Not yet, but I'll let them know when they get home from work."

He paused for a split second. I thought I had him, but I was wrong again.

"Ok then, hop in the car and I'll take you home; I don't want you guys to get in trouble out here."

"We won't get in any trouble," I quickly replied.

"Yes, I know you are good kids, but someone else may stop you and they may not understand the way I do, so I'll take you myself, unless you'd rather I just lock you up."

"No! No! You don't have to do that," I shouted. I was about to take off and make a run for it, just before he said,

"By the way, Fred Easter, how's your dad, J.C., doing."

The jig was up as he had hit me with a gut shot that paralyzed me. My stomach dropped and at the same time I was visualizing a whooping that was certainly in my near future.

"I'm sorry I'm sorry, I won't ever do this again, just don't tell my Daddy!"

"Get in the car, Fred, and you boys get in too."

We all slowly got into the police car. No one said a word, there was no time for me to talk. I was busy trying to compose another brilliant idea of how to avoid this whooping that I know was well on the way. Even my imagination couldn't compose an idea in my own head that seemed anywhere near feasible enough change my inevitable fate with my father.

I didn't realize it then, but this officer who knew my father was doing me and my friends a favor by taking us home to our parents. He was just another part of the community that cared about our future. I didn't understand that then, as a matter of fact, I thought he was a horrible guy, but I wish there were more like him in today's world.

I don't want anyone to think that I long for the communities of yesteryear, because that would not be true. I know as well as anyone that those days are long gone, never to return. Not only that, but you can't take the good in an era without bringing the bad along too, and the comfort of those days does not outweigh the progress that we've made as a people since then. I probably don't know eight people that live on my block today, as opposed to knowing everyone on my block when I grew up, but back then we had almost no communication with anyone *outside* of our immediate community, unless there were unusual circumstances.

Today things are so different for kids in the way their communities connect and interact. Due to the availability of social media, which has changed so much of our daily lives, young people have friends from everywhere, not just within their zip code. Their worlds are in ways vastly bigger as they can connect with friends from virtually anywhere.

SOCIAL PROGRAMS

We can't clearly understand how our neighborhoods became so dysfunctional without recognizing the devastating impact of some of the social programs intended to help. In 1935

President Franklin D. Roosevelt introduced the Social Security Act, which was comprised of two key social safety net programs. One gave aid to families that suffered the loss of income in the household due to death, injury or incapacitation of the bread winner, and the second provided a Social Security benefit to older American citizens to prevent a slide into poverty at retirement.

Title IV of the act created Aid to Dependent Children, which was renamed Aid to Families with Dependent Children (AFDC) in 1962 by the Kennedy Administration. The program was initially designed during the depression by Roosevelt to offer aid to poor parents, at the time presumed to be single women caring for children in the home who were absent a husband due to death or abandonment. How this program was administered in later years, however, ultimately caused even greater hardship for Black families. Through what came to be known as the "man in the house" rule, social workers could make unannounced visits to the homes of mothers with children to search for evidence of an adult male living with or even effectively dating the mother. If a man was found in the home, the children stood to lose their financial assistance. Though struck down by the Supreme Court in 1968, this moralistic interpretation of Title IV attempted to enshrine social judgements about who was entitled to assistance and who was not. That was not, the

Supreme Court ruled, an original intention of the law.

Section 8 of Roosevelt's Housing Act of 1937 also established subsidized housing for women and children. The modern program was authorized by Congress in 1974 under the Department of Housing and Urban Development. The fact that aid to dependent children and housing assistance were both tied to poor mothers served to empower women in poor Black households and disenfranchise the fathers, often willing but unable to secure meaningful work. In most cases, his shelter and his children's income depended on the mother's ability to secure aid in his absence. It was for a long while routine for poor Black women to evict the men in their lives at a moment's notice to avoid the social worker. This created a strained and uneasy power dynamic in poor Black households. Thus, the slow exodus of Black fathers from poor children's homes began. Interestingly, the stigma of the absent Black father has falsely become associated with Black people of all social strata, though that was never really the case for working class or middle-class Black families. The fact that the male head of household was disappearing in poor children's lives, however, would create a whole new set of problems for impoverished Black communities.

The man in the house rule was particularly devastating and demoralizing. Many fathers lived month to month essentially in hiding within their own homes, sneaking out back doors at the first sign of an investigation. This ridiculous set of circumstances led to an erosion of respect for the men in poor households. That loss of respect often settled into resentment on all sides. For the impoverished Black father, his circumstances became a near surgical decapitation of his pride and worthiness. The man unable to meet social obligations for his family through employment, education or advancement—all lacking in many cases through no fault of his own—faced his family feeling small and dejected, cut off from them in ways literal and figurative.

  This search for men in poor women's households became a normal practice that seemed to be a game between social workers and poor families. Sometimes the social workers would come with an assistant to monitor the back doors while they knocked on the front. Grown men resorted to hiding in closets and under beds.

As one could imagine, this led to the breakup of families that were already living on the brink of collapse due to joblessness, poverty, and hunger. Then came the phrase adopted by a lot of poor Black women, "I don't need no help, I can do bad all by myself". As cute and hip as this may have sounded, it really served to deepen the divide between men and their families, which caused irreparable damage that would trickle down through the generations.

Make no mistake about it, when a man's respect is taken away in his home, it will most certainly carry over to all aspects of his being, because the stink of that vileness is recognized by everyone he encounters. This is a lonely, deep, dark place to be in, which is why so many Black men sank deeper into lives of misery and regret, finding escape through other means.

The goal for some men became to refuse to accept this diminished role; to lift themselves out of the cold, cold spot they found themselves in one way or another. Some choose hard work and learned to accept and be proud of their humble station in life, while others choose work and education and edged their way to a better life.

Then you have those that refused to accept a life of mediocrity and decided *not* to work. That choice often resulted in a life of crime spent lived on the margins. Some that choose this route became financially successful and in some respects, pillars of their community. In fact, that man's reasoning is not so hard to understand, because he adopts the attitude of, *"I'll do what I got to do to make good things happen for my kids."* Don't get it confused, many that choose this path won't stay true to their original intent. For various reasons, they end up a victim to their vices. Drug use is rampant, along with the eventual erosion of their morals and principles.

Often, these men die a tragic death at a young age. Some commit violent crimes and are sentenced to long prison terms. Others become repeat offenders in the penal system, where they eventually meet a few of those guys on the margins that they admired in their youth.

I, myself, fell victim to more than nineteen years of drug abuse and a life of crime that landed me in and out of prison in three different states. In one of my years between incarceration, I found myself in a direct confrontation with the unjust "man in the house" rule. I hadn't heard of it until that day.

At the time, my lady, Lisa, and I were living in St. Louis on Oakland Ave., not far from Forest Park. We had three kids, the two oldest were eight and nine, and were not my biological children. The baby was my child and was only a year old. The kids weren't at home, and I had just come home after a day of hustling, which was an everyday routine for me. I was tired and I had just laid down when I heard a knock on the door.

"I'll get it," Lisa shouted.

"Okay," I said.

Before I could comfortably adjust the pillow under my head, Lisa ran into the room and stood over me and whispered in my ear, "Fred, you've got to go out the back door for a minute"

"What?"

"Just step out on the back porch, for a few

minutes."

"What's wrong?"

"The case worker for my welfare is at the door, and if she sees you, they will take me off."

"Open the damn door and let her in now, or I will," I told her, with a tone that could easily be heard through the door.

"What are you trying to do to us?" But before she could finish her plea, I opened the door and there stood a White lady who seemed to be about 30 or 35 years of age, kind of cute, with a puzzled look on her face.

"Who are you?" she asked,

"Who are you" I asked her right back.

"I'm the social worker and I'm here for a visit, which is my job to make sure that there are no violations in the household."

"And what would be a violation?"

"You could be," She quickly replied, with a voice filled with authority.

Lisa stood to the side in total disbelief, not knowing what the outcome would be.

"Well, I'll tell you now, I'm not a violation. My name is Fred Easter and I live here. We're doing everything we can to take care of these kids and it damn sho ain't easy, but if you want to make it worse for us, go right ahead and do what you got to do."

The lady looked at me unperturbed, and she didn't give any facial indication that would prepare us for what she said next.

"Mr. Easter, you don't have to worry about me coming by unannounced ever again," she said as she turned to leave.

"Have a good day, sir."

She quickly closed the door and went down the stairs. We watched her as she got into her car and pulled off. I didn't know what in the hell had just happened and neither did Lisa, but we knew that it wouldn't be long before we would know something. I spent the next twenty minutes hugging Lisa, trying to reassure her that we would be ok, regardless of if she remained on welfare or not. It was unbelievable, but we never heard from that social worker again.

After I thought about that confrontation later, I think I came to understand the look I saw in her eyes. It gave me a newfound respect for some of these social workers who were forced to participate in these family separations, which was what the job entailed at the time. This lady was not proud of the part that she played in separating families; it seemed to me she knew the man was truly needed in the house.

The impact of fathers intentionally being removed from their homes through poor social program execution was tragic. We may never accurately measure the full impact because there are so many layers to this travesty that are never talked about. But the next phenomenon to remove poor Black men from the home would have a corporate profit motive as driver. Enter the prison industrial complex. The privatization of the penal system was the next catastrophe about to hit poor Black communities.

Businesses with deep pockets are always willing to pay off local governments to exert their will on poor communities. No single business has been as devastating to the lives of poor Black families as the industry created to incarcerate and warehouse Black men. The buildings within our prison industrial complex can be torn down when we're ready to move on from this terrible idea. But how will neighborhoods ever recover from the virtual disappearance of all of the working-age Black men from poor neighborhoods all over the country?

The disproportionate number of Black men facing high mortality rates and mass incarceration have forced Black women to take extreme measures to compensate and search for balance in their lives.

For some women, trying to achieve a sense of normalcy meant trying to preserve family relationships through bars as the children looked on. For other women, the lack of available Black men in the neighborhood might mean you date and fall in love with men already behind bars. Both of these situations in my opinion, have cast a giant shadow of confusion on the children of this era, as these men, spoken of but absent, were almost revered from the child's point of view.

Thanks to some unintentionally misconstrued messaging, prison life has been glorified for some of these kids who've heard of these imprisoned father figures almost like legends. Many of these kids become victims themselves due to their urge to imitate the dysfunctional learned behavior of the men that their moms have brought into their lives. Combined with high unemployment, a lack of education, and the low bar set as a result of these ill-fated relationships, it seems many of these kids are headed on a road to eventual incarceration. Unless we do something to address the health of poor neighborhoods, we're just waiting for the next step in a long slow genocide to begin.

HEALTHCARE

Healthcare, or the lack thereof, is yet another way in which government gets to influence the strength or weakness of communities. Because of the enormous amounts of money made by insurance companies, pharmaceutical companies, and all other links in the healthcare food chain, the poor are at the mercy of conglomerates. Those who can afford platinum plans have access to some of the best care in the world while everyone else subsists on what they can afford at the time.

This competition for healthcare amongst the classes exists because we refuse to think for ourselves. We depend too much on the messages from our elected officials who, for the most part, have been bought and paid for by special interests. Corruption like a virus has invaded all levels of government and eroded the protections put in place for the people. Rather than advocate for a healthcare system more like what the rest of the developed world has, our politicians stay on message with ridiculous misinformation and untruths about the cost of healthcare and socialism, despite the urgent needs of their own constituents.

During the 2016 election campaign, I listened to a Trump supporter in Kentucky being interviewed by an MSNBC reporter. The question asked of her was, *"How do you feel about Obamacare?"*

"I don't like it, and they need to get rid of it because that Obamacare is hurting everybody," she said.

She was then asked what insurance she had, and how did she feel about her own insurance plan. She went on to give a testimonial about how good her insurance had been for her and so many other people that she knew of in Kentucky. As it turned out, this lady's insurance plan was Kentucky Health Plan, United Health Care Community Plan, which is a Medicare and Medicaid Health Plan. This is the Affordable Care Act, better known as

Obamacare, the same plan that she so vigorously denounced only moments before. This lady's uninformed response is not unusual for the low-information voter, basing their opinions on the talking points of their favorite partisan idols. She's been willingly deceived; encouraged to accept an interpretation of news that confirms her world view, even if that world view is shaped in part by bigotry. She will happily vote against her own interests (vote away her own healthcare!) to stick it to Obama. Voters manipulated by blinding hatred of the other guy have been voting against their best interest for decades, even for life and death matters like healthcare.

Voters are bombarded by voices on all sides of the healthcare issue. Some politicians have been remarkably successful at promoting the position of the highest bidder. How do they make these claims seem legitimate? With studies and reports demonstrating what great harm will befall the American people if we offer healthcare as a human right like the rest of the industrialized world. Here are a few of the talking points used to sour the American public on good healthcare policy.

1. This would create Socialism, which robs individuals of the ability to choose their own insurance plan or doctors.
2. This new system would eventually erode the quality of healthcare because there would be too many patients for doctors to

service and still provide a high level of care.
3. The deficit will explode and this great financial burden would be placed on the backs of our children—our children!
4. It's not fair for the working class and more affluent to pay for the healthcare of those that want a handout.
5. Most doctors don't get paid in a timely fashion and their amount of pay would decrease, which would have a profound effect on the dedication of doctors.
6. This lower pay would deplete the pool of future qualified doctors, who will opt out to choose more lucrative professions.
7. Last but not least, healthcare for everyone would raise taxes.

Despite the opposition's drumbeat on these and other reasons to avoid a public health plan, those who are looking for real information can find the following.
1. Preventive care would decrease the number of surgeries, which would save money for all involved.
2. Healthcare for all would save lives almost immediately.
3. Healthcare for all would have a powerful, positive impact on the small businesses who couldn't afford healthcare for their employees.

4. Because of this, small businesses growth would boom, and millions of new jobs would be created.
5. Treatment for patients would be faster because insurance companies wouldn't need to approve all services.
6. Families would not go broke because of pre-existing conditions.
7. Because every working person would pay something into healthcare, it would be more affordable for everyone.
8. I've added my own idea, that I believe could be a bonus that would solve one of the sticking points for a lot of people. Create three levels of care, so that those that choose to can pay an additional amount that would enable them to choose their own doctor in any network. This cost could still be less than what they pay now.
9. All communities would be better prepared for pandemics because everyone would already be covered, which could save thousands of lives.

The type of care suggested in the bullets above could be provided to everyone. I still believe that the people who've been fortunate enough to earn a much better income should have broader options—more choice on care providers perhaps.

There are so many good ideas to explore that are all better than the options we have now. As good as the Affordable Care Act has been for the millions previously without coverage, it still came up enormously short of what healthcare in America should look like.

Lack of decent prescription coverage has wreaked havoc on communities throughout the country too. Treacherous over pricing has left many families deciding whether to eat or buy insulin. In some cases, there is a truly thin wall between life and death. In other instances, people are scraping and sacrificing to buy drugs their doctors have been pushed to offer by pharmaceutical reps. That's part of the rip off, too.

The cheat is so deep that it would be nearly impossible to reform this system as it exists today. I propose a complete dismantling of healthcare as we know it with a new construction similar to that proposed by Bernie Sanders with elements of the Affordable Care Act and a few of the suggestions above.

SCHOOL BUSING

School busing at the time of its inception, seemed necessary because of the vast difference in the quality of education in different communities. But evolution has proved to be needed in all walks of life, even in education.

Americans spent billions of dollars busing

elementary and secondary school students to and from schools outside of their own communities. Instead of transporting our most prized possessions to other communities, Black communities wondered, what would happen if we invest that money in our own neighborhoods by providing better housing, nutrition and modern schools equipped with the technology to prepare *all* kids for the stiff competition that lies ahead?

ADVANTAGES OF ELIMINATING BUSING
1. With better funding, we would be able to attract more qualified, dedicated teachers with better pay to neighborhood schools in Black communities.
2. These same teachers would have the luxury of teaching children with a better attention span, instead of trying to force feed information to kids that are already worn out from unnecessary time on school busses.
3. Parents with limited funds and time have a better opportunity to attend school functions such as parent teacher meetings and other programs that help to bond families with their child's school community.
4. Parents get a better opportunity to know each other, which helps create a village of support for parents and students.
5. Top athletic recruits would have an opportunity to play sports in their own communities, which infuses pride and respect in communities that need

it desperately.

I recently talked to my daughter Rukiya, who is grown now, about her experience of riding the school bus in her early years in the public-school system. She reminded me that her day started at 5:00 am every morning so that she could catch a school bus that would get her to school around 7:15 am. She rode from St. Louis to Eureka, Missouri, which is more than 27 miles one way, all throughout her elementary and secondary education.

She also shared with me that even though she was in a better system, the way she was treated by fellow students and the school's staff, was hugely different than the treatment the other students received. Busing was a trade-off for our kids which meant they often felt like second class citizens in their new school communities. Black kids bore the brunt of alienation and loneliness for a chance at a better education. White parents and Black parents alike remained skeptical at this imperfect solution and ultimately, the courts whittled away at desegregation laws until there was practically nothing left.

ADVANTAGES OF SCHOOL BUSING

The biggest advantages of school busing may have been the fact that it seemed to work.

According to Richard Kahlenberg, senior fellow at the Century Foundation, a think tank that supports integration, "Desegregation was highly successful. It provided a way to raise academic achievement for African Americans that was far more successful than anything we've tried since."

In fact, after busing desegregation was already being dismantled by the courts, the evidence was just beginning to emerge from decades-long studies to show that busing improved outcomes for Black students, with no harm to White students.

The evidence was too late to save a program that was demonized by White parents nearly universally and viewed skeptically by Black parents as well.

Yes, there were a few advantages of school busing, but, in my view, it was another tool for division that stripped poor communities of some of their strengths.

THE DIVISION CAUSED BY DRUGS

Although drugs are not the root of division in America, it has certainly been used in a sort of genius-like way to deepen the divide in several categories of our everyday life. Drugs are eroding the fabric of everyday life for poor communities everywhere, both Black and White.

It would be hard to match the devotion that drug users have for their drug of choice. They will treat people with total contempt and respond with loving devotion for their crutch. This devil, like a slave master, only takes and never gives. Drugs demand more and more of the user, until eventually it asks that you give up even your hopes and dreams. So conniving is the drug, that the user doesn't even see the decline, while others can see it so clearly.

Seeing it still doesn't give the loving witnesses in your life the ability to stop or slow the destruction. This portion of my life's journey was full of darkness, but I was able to escape.

While writing this passage, my brother Harry Easter immediately came to mind because he was dedicated to self-destruction more earnestly than anyone I'd ever known except perhaps me. When I look back on that period, it's almost like an out of body experience that makes me shiver.

We weren't what you would call hustling partners, probably because our familiarity with one another didn't allow either of us the opportunity to exploit the other, which, in my mind, would have been unproductive for the both of us. I can vividly remember a conversation that we had, while we both were high and feeling good and invincible. We talked about ideas we both had for getting some money, which, as I can remember, was the topic of most of our talks.

The views that he was sharing seemed to make a lot of sense, then suddenly he stopped talking, stood up, and began to pivot back and forth as if he were about to lose his balance. His eyes were closed, and I knew he was good and high—I was too! But I wasn't ready for what he was about to say.

"Bro," he said.

I heard him, but I didn't respond. It didn't matter—he wasn't looking for a response.

"Bro," he said again, and then continued on, "If God made anything better than this, He must have kept it for Himself," he said referring to heroin.

"You got that right," I responded.

At that time, I didn't realize the enormity of what we had just sanctioned, regardless of its foolishness. We both know now what we didn't know then. We were sinking fast.

Euphoria is a state of intense excitement and happiness that causes you to have a great urge to repeat the act or thing that brought this feeling about in the first place. Simply being able to bring home a decent paycheck to your family can be a source of joy and happiness. Food smells, anticipation, money, even a person can give you that type of joy on occasion.

But nothing brings about euphoria as intense and rapidly as drugs, which is why the use of illegal drugs has become so prevalent and in demand in poor communities.

It's no accident that the communities hit the hardest by this drug epidemic, have also been the most poverty stricken. These neighborhoods have proven to be the most vulnerable, pertaining to the influx of drugs, because they lack any real representation by the people whose job it is to protect the communities. Corrupt politicians and police are only a few that contribute to this mix. There are so many more sources of frustration in these neighborhoods: unemployment, hunger, poor living conditions, undeserving role models, struggling overworked single parents, poor education and the loss of hope spells poverty.

This broad mix of social challenges is the perfect recipe for a self-inflicted genocide. Self-medicating with illicit drugs is how people in terrible situations get back to euphoria. You must escape the lack of opportunity, the violence, the PTSD that no one is treating. You must be tough to make it out on the other side. Despite all of the daily obstacles, there are many success stories.

There are many side-hustle occupations in the hood that get varying degrees of respect; some honest, some dishonest. But even the pimps, players, thieves and drug dealers often protect and recognize the special talents in the neighborhood. It's not uncommon to see a street entrepreneur with their arms around a talented young person, not to harass them but to protect and advise them. Everyone sees the missed opportunities in their own rear view. The men and women in these communities live vicariously through the kids with potential and a real shot to make it out alive.

Everyone wants to have a hand in their success story. When they reach their highest potential, the entire community comes along for the ride.

Just the thought of some of my own encounters like these is enough to warm my heart. But of course, we also know how to play the numbers, and the cold hard reality is that for every one that makes it out, thousands stumble and fall into the grasp of failure and lost hopes; searching for euphoria in all the wrong places, because they couldn't get a foothold on a way up and out.

When our young people manage to avoid the hard drugs, they often still embrace marijuana. This lesser vice has been the wall between employment and unemployment in a lot of cases, because drug tests deter many folks from even filling out an application.

Meanwhile the real criminals continue to flood our neighborhoods with poison. Their victims have been groomed from day one to succumb to the same systemic problems that were waiting for their fathers: prison, mental illness, homelessness and early, violent death. If the dealers are ever caught, most often they receive a slap on the wrist due to their connections in high places and their ability to grease the palms of the right people.

PRESCRIPTION DRUGS AND ALCOHOL

The desire for some to paint a difference between their own shortcomings and others is a convenient way of deflecting an undesirable picture of themselves. This explains why prescription drug users and those that partake in a drink of the good stuff, can so easily look down their noses at those that use street drugs with contempt and disdain. The presumption is that legal drugs are less damaging than illegal, but that belief can come back to bite unsuspecting hypocrites. They usually discover in the long run that legal drug abuse is just as damaging, if not more so.

Because of the societal acceptance of legal drugs and alcohol, along with its abundance and availability, abuse can happen in plain sight. I doubt that there is any family that has not suffered in some way from this epidemic of prescription drug abuse.

I had a front row view as a child of the devastating effects of alcoholism. I remember the love and pain my Aunt Arlena felt as she tried to pump pride and respectability into her only child, Edward, while he pursued escape through a bottle. He was helpless and drunk day by day and she was powerless to change that.

Not a day went by that Aunt Arlena didn't have his clothes cleaned and pressed so that he could leave the house looking the part of a distinguished and successful man. By the time he made his way back home at the end of the day, he would stumble back into her arms, his safe haven.

He didn't start out like this. His was a long slow devolution that delivered him from the threshold of prosperity to the hands of drunkenness.

People begin the use of alcohol or any other addiction for lots of different reasons; a death in the family, unemployment, stress. A little helps them get through the day when they just can't cope with the daily grind that life presents. The drink so often leads to drugs to enhance that good feeling that grows dimmer without increased consumption.

These drug addictions may include opioids, like oxycodone, hydrocodone, OxyContin and even heroin. And more often than, these drugs do not replace one another but are used in conjunction in order to bring about a more intense high. Anyone of these combinations can cause severe health problems or death.

If at some point, an addict realizes that a change is needed, they can seek help through Narcotics Anonymous (NA) or Alcoholics Anonymous (AA). These programs have had amazing success with aiding addicts in recovery. They should be applauded for the great work they do to resurrect addicts and their families. It's amazing how many different roads lead back to the same path. Now that an opioid crisis has gripped parts of poor White America, it provides us with another kick in the butt to remind us just how much we have in common. The destruction of drugs and alcohol has no boundaries, no color lines, and no respect for any class.

Not Perfectly Divided

CHAPTER IV
RELIGIOUS DIVIDE

MAN CREATED RELIGION

What's the one true religion? When did it start and who started it? Every group of modern humans on earth have their own origin story. Some may lay claim to the same Alpha and Omega that I do. No evidence can be taken as fact, especially since some religions are thousands of years old.

I don't know about you, but I find it difficult to keep a story straight after a few minutes, especially if it's coming from the mouth of man. Even if confirmed with written documentation, that still doesn't guarantee truth. I'm not accusing anyone, or any organization, of intentionally being dishonest with their interpretation of their own teachings as to when, where, and how their religion began.

I do know that two different people can hear or read the same story and still have two completely different interpretations of what was said. It's the same with religion.

Religious organizations are some of the world's most powerful and wealthy institutions. That was true thousands of years ago and is even truer today. Ministers can begin to feel the call to pursue fortune and fame. Many have righteous intent that results in a lot of good.

THE STRUGGLE

By now you're probably thinking that I'm an atheist, but nothing could be further from the truth. God has granted me the privilege of living long enough to see some amazing things and I am grateful. Not only that, but my thirst for knowledge keeps me searching for answers to impossible questions. I don't have to know all of the answers right away.

On July 17, 2020, the world took a deep breath followed by a long pause because of the death of two icons in the Civil Rights Movement. John Lewis, who died at the age of 80, and C. T. Vivian, who was 95 at the time of his death, both passed on. Though they've departed this plane, their work's impact will forever be felt throughout the world in the hearts and souls of all people that truly desire real freedom, voting rights and equal justice across the board, regardless of creed, color or place of origin.

It's amazing that these two men that lived such parallel lives to one another as ministers in their fight for justice, and in their studies at the same school to achieve their degree in theology, left together as well. They both marched alongside the Rev. Dr. Martin Luther King Jr. and they departed this world on the same day.

What a sad and bittersweet loss. Their faith in God provided them both with the resolve to keep working to the last for freedom's cause, always as instruments of peace. A witness like theirs makes it hard to understand the viciousness and hatred displayed by men of one faith against another in Gods' name.

GOD HAS NO RELIGION OR GENDER

Contrary to the belief of most; God is not religious, nor does God have a gender. Furthermore, this thinking seems to be the root of countless problems throughout the world, since the beginning of man in the flesh. We all have our own personal relationship with God because God is in each one of us, but this doesn't mean that God is our personal servant. I thought we were servants of God and not the other way around! Like everything else, man has confused this concept, too. The confusion doesn't stop there, the confusion only grows within us, but God is not confused. The more I learn, the more discomfort that comes over me when I hear people refer to God as "him," "he" and sometimes, "the big fella," along with other pronouns that cannot nearly describe this greatness that is the Creator of everything.

The universe, along with all that this infinite greatness encompasses, not excluding all the different people that occupy this wondrous world, were made by God, the creator of all things. Even the winds that possess the power to blow all earthly belongings away in the blink of an eye, the waters that can wash the land away into nothingness and fire that can scorch the earth to ruins is God's to command. This power does not come at the hands of him, he or big fella, and thank God, it doesn't.

MY POSITION

My faith in God has been and will always remain unshakeable, but my belief in man is measured by his works and deeds and not by his words. Man's words attempt to paint a connection between God and religion in one broad stroke, while claiming that our desires are in fact, God's will. Just the fact that God was responsible for our birth and breath makes it almost impossible to ever separate one from the other. All of the unbelievable situations that God has pulled us through are *more* than confirmation enough to deepen and implant the teaching that one doesn't exist without the other.

I have no problem with specific religious teachings if no one gets hurt while in the process of practicing the teachings of their chosen path of worship. What I don't like is the audacity of the righteous of any religion to proclaim that my belief is ungodly because my belief differs from theirs. God is bigger than that!

My earliest memories in life are filled with the indoctrination into the world of church and religion. I know now that some of my teachings in church were the same as most churches, but some were different in some pretty radical ways. Some of these differences is what stands out the most to me and has proven to have a profound effect as to who I am today.

CHURCH RULES

I was raised in a church known as Rising Star Missionary Baptist Church at 3424 LaSalle St. in St. Louis, Missouri. My mother, Marie Easter, made sure that I never missed a Sunday of worship and praise. My father, Julius Easter, believed in God but he didn't go to church. Therefore, he didn't intervene in church business unless some matter had gotten totally out of hand.

I only witnessed this intervention once in my life. In my early years there, the pastor was Reverend Sherman Glover. I remember him as a tall man that always seemed to be serious and intimidating. My oldest brother, Harry Easter, joined the church for the purpose of appeasing our mother. This caused him to be pulled in two different directions, because he would now have to obey the rules of the church, which proved to be too demanding. He will occasionally reminisce with me about his encounters with Reverend Glover.

Harry always became animated when describing the fear and the intimidation that he felt, just from the presence of this man. Keep in mind that Harry was born in 1941, therefore his years as an adolescent or teenager was in the late 40s and 50s, and television was relatively new. Reverend Glover imposed rules on the members of the church that seemed to be irrational and barbaric.

For example, he didn't want members to watch television (he called it a foolish box) and he didn't want the kids to play sports (this too was classified as foolish and unnecessary). If these rules were not adhered to, the violator could be expelled from the church. Not only that, but once expelled the only way to have your membership revived was to show humility. This was done by standing in front of the church congregation on Sunday and asking for forgiveness for the sins that you've committed. Forgiveness was most often given, but the thought of having to do this was deterrent enough to cause the members to hide some of their most desired activities, or totally discontinue them.

THE PLAYGROUND

In my early years until I was ten years of age when we lived at 2222 Rutger St. Reverend Glover and his wife lived at 2303. The playground known as the Sunshine Laundry Lot was where all the kids in our neighborhood played baseball and football, along with other games. The movie screen was on this lot also and all the kids came there twice a week to see movies. In other words, this was the center of fun times for kids, but it was directly across the street from Reverend Glover's house, who forbade all those activities.

He would sit in the yard in the front of the house where he could see everybody who played on the lot. The weight on the church members as a result of these rules that forbade practically any fun time, proved to be a tremendous strain on Harry. Our uncle, Luke Easter, was one of the first professional African American baseball players, playing for the Cleveland Indians.

Harry wanted so badly to be like Uncle Luke because of all the love, admiration and respect that everyone had for him. Luke Easter was raised in this neighborhood, and he was a hero to these people. His accomplishments were renowned. Harry wanted that same adoration; to round the bases just like him.

His fear, however, seemed to override his desires most of the time. So, Harry didn't get to play ball very often in front of the Reverend's house. Until the day my father intervened.

Whenever Harry would tell this story, he would get so animated. He was always a good storyteller, but he would become even more dramatic when he described the first time that our father allowed him to play ball in the presence of Reverend Glover.

This is how he describes that unforgettable experience. Harry was standing down the street from the playing field, watching the other kids play baseball, afraid to play with them because the preacher was sitting in the front yard, watching like a hawk. All of a sudden, out of nowhere, our dad pulled up in his car alongside Harry and shouted out,

"Why aren't you playing ball, Harry?"

"Because Reverend Glover won't let me."

"What the hell do you mean he won't let you?"

"I'm not supposed to play baseball because of his rules."

My dad quickly parked the car and got out. At the same time reminding Harry, with a voice loud enough so everyone present, including Reverend Glover, could hear his announcement.

"Glover ain't your daddy! **I'm** your daddy, boy, now get on up there and play ball."

Harry couldn't believe his ears! He proceeded to the playing field, a little reluctantly for a moment, peering over at the preacher to check his demeanor.

"Go on," my dad urged him, as he got closer and closer to the field. It seemed as though with every step the fear evaporated from his body until he finally became more confident in dad. It wasn't long before Harry began running toward his teammates with an expression of joy and excitement. Once the other kids realized what had happened, they allowed Harry to take the position that he wanted. The game quickly resumed and all the kids, including Harry, had a great time playing. Dad continued to watch with joy while the kids had a great time.

As I recall the story, Harry even stuck out his chest while facing the preacher, as the preacher sat and watched. Wow! This was unbelievable. The preacher never said a word and from the sound of Harrys voice, this is certainly a moment that will forever be etched into his memory as one of his proudest recollections of our father. As joyful as this moment was, it would not be long lived, because on the days that followed when dad wasn't around, Harry reverted back to his previous state of fear while in the presence of the preacher. But he didn't have to ask the church for forgiveness.

I'm almost thirteen years younger than Harry, and Reverend Glover was getting older. Therefore, his presence wasn't quite as intimidating in my teenage years. This still didn't dispel the clear understanding to me that Reverend Glover's relationship with the members of the church was strange, because he seemed to be loved and feared by all the members, including the men. I won't claim the feeling of love, but the fear was certainly passed on to me and all of the other kids that I knew of at the church.

Reverend Glover's sermons weren't contained to the pulpit. He was masterful in his ability to slowly move throughout the church. As he moved around, everyone seemed to feel as though he was looking directly at them, as his coarse, thunderous voice seemed to ring from the heavens—and this was without the use of a microphone. Occasionally, he would call someone out, with that thunderous voice,

"You, you right there, you ain't got nothing! You need to be born again."

In this church, being born again meant that you gained faith with Jesus and a connection with God. Some churches only require that you come to the front of the church and announce that you accept Jesus Christ as your Lord and Savior. The conversion process was a lot different at Rising Star.

Once someone decided to get converted, they would then come forward and sit on the first pew in the center of the church, which was called the Moaner's Bench. Every eye in the church would immediately be focused on the person sitting on the Moaner's Bench. It wouldn't take long before the preacher would instruct the person that hoped to become a member of the church to hold their head back and look up and call out, "Lord have mercy" or "thank you, Jesus!" He might touch his head, while emphatically urging the person to call "Mercy," louder and louder. This repeated chant would continue until the preacher saw some sign of change in the sound or movement of the person. At that time, the preacher would pronounce that he or she had been born again.

I have a vivid recollection of Reverend Glover proclaiming time and time again that if your conversion wasn't brought about in this manner, you hadn't truly received Jesus. Not only that, but you could only get this deliverance at Rising Star. Without this you were going to Hell! At the age of nine I, too, was converted at the same church but under the leadership of a different pastor. His name was Reverend Andrew Smith. His style was totally different, but his results were just as magnificent, as far as his ability to impact the lives of many in a positive manner. I never heard him denounce other churches' connection with God, but the thought of my early teachings never left my mind.

Because of this, I could never understand how God could be so cold, that he could only accept members from Rising Star into the pearly gates of heaven. It just never made sense to me. Regardless of my apprehensions, my reverence for Reverend Smith never wavered, because I knew that he was a man full of love and understanding. Not only that, but he also helped me in so many ways. I received help from him years after my time as a member of his church had ended. That, and the times that I witnessed how he uplifted many others, will forever enable me to feel ingratiated and thankful for his presence in my life. I loved him. My thirst for answers concerning religion never left me, but my faith in God is stronger than ever.

DIFFERENT PRAYERS TO ONE GOD

Prayer is an act that establishes a direct line of communication with God. Through this communication we establish a greater inner strength, which can catapult us all to greater heights in any capacity. But so often prayer is viewed as some type of mystical phenomenon that will render us free of all our problems and guarantee satisfaction in all that we desire. This attitude can and will fail.

My experience with prayer is that it must be accompanied with desire, a plan, and hard work. Without this combination, prayer doesn't have a chance, and neither do those that continue to practice the mHre futile method. We must also keep in mind that someone else's prayer may be the exact opposite of what you pray for. Therefore, your work must outweigh the work and endurance of the opposition.

This opposition in prayers and hard work is the very reason why our quest for justice and equality has lasted so long. It's no accident that we are still fighting the same fight that our forefathers and mothers fought, and that we still find ourselves in the same fight right now. We must understand that the Klan and other hate organizations continue to work just as hard as we do, to assure that we never have equality or justice. Not only that, but the opposition that I talk about, shows its ugly face in some of the most influential positions of power in the private and public sector. That's right, we have elected public officials that pray and work on plans, every day, to keep us down.

On this day of July 29, 2020, I find it almost impossible to continue writing because I've been compelled to watch the ceremony of the great Freedom Fighter, John Lewis. This is his ceremonial last escort from Washington, DC, as they proceed to Atlanta, Georgia, where he served for decades as a true dedicated fighter for a better world.

As the procession draws near an end, I am constantly reminded of the story that his brother Henry Grant Lewis told about a moment the two shared. The way he described it was quite subtle but powerful. He explained that John was being sworn into Congress. As his brothers and sisters sat in the gallery above, Lewis paused, looked up, and gave a thumbs up. At the proceedings that followed, Henry asked John what he had been thinking when he flashed the thumbs up.

"I was thinking, this is a long way from the cotton fields of Alabama," he said.

This exodus from those cotton fields was no accident, but was realized as a result of prayer, hard work and an unrelenting determination that remained in him until he took his last breath.

As the hearse drove away, it was kind of ironic, that Republican and Democratic politicians gathered and spoke with one another as if in perfect harmony, while giving John Lewis his last and final farewell. This superficial display of togetherness would soon dissipate, just as soon as both parties returned to their assigned partisan corners.

CHURCH AND STATE: NOT CLOSE

Through a good friend of mine, Daryl Davis, I had the pleasure of meeting Pastor B. T. Rice of New Horizon Seventh Day Christian Church of St Louis. I also met Dr. Barry Black, the 62nd chaplain of the United States Senate. Daryl invited me to his church a few years ago to listen to Dr. Black speak. From my under-standing, he visits New Horizon Church at least once a year, because of his close relationship with Pastor Rice. From the very first time, I heard him speak, I knew I wanted to hear more of what he had to offer concerning life and the word of God. Since then, I've read all his books, which have given me a different outlook in regard to some of my thinking.

After reading his stories, I came away with a new view on his purpose and determination to make a difference in this world. I felt that his path was righteous, every step of the way. Like us all, he has his weaknesses, but he desires to do right and make a difference, in a positive way. Because of this, each day, prior to the start of Donald Trump's impeachment hearings, Dr. Black would give a prayer. I'm sure each prayer was well thought out and targeted at those who needed it most. The Republican Senators and all who sat in those chambers held the fate of the country in their hands. But an ear to hear was not in the building. Therefore, the unjust decision of these Senators to not even vote to hear the case was proof enough to me that church and state are miles apart. Regardless of this, and other obvious infractions by those in power, I will not give up on the state. Because I know ***we can*** change things if we unite. And I'll never give up on God.

Not Perfectly Divided

CHAPTER V
POLITICAL DIVIDE

THE SOUL OF THE NATION

Sound the alarm! I mean it, ***sound the alarm***! This madness we're living in is unbelievable and unrecognizable. Our country is in the midst of a once in a century pandemic. At no point in history has there been more technology and resources available to control a pandemic than now. However, the Trump administration, playing politics, has chosen not to utilize the basic tools and common-sense science available to us to help mitigate this virus.

At the time of this writing, there are almost five million reported coronavirus cases and more than 154,000 deaths. Still, there is no national plan to control or rid ourselves of this vicious MONSTER! ***WHAT IN THE HELL IS WRONG WITH THESE PEOPLE?!?!***

Congressional Democrats approved a plan to stimulate the economy with the $3.5 trillion Hero's Act, which would provide a temporary lifeline for those in need. If passed, it would support families and businesses. Funding could and would help resuscitate the economy and prevent the evictions of millions of families, while allowing small businesses to remain hopeful. If the money is distributed equitably instead of allowing the wealthy to dig their hands deep into the coffers

Not Perfectly Divided

first, we could even strike a blow against the growing wealth divide, preventing those in need from sinking deeper into depression and despair. At the time of this writing, the United States has lost more than 40 million jobs; that does not include jobs lost prior to the pandemic.

A few months ago, millions of good, hard working people who were doing just fine, began adjusting to a new reality of near homelessness and food lines. The same people who might have stood in line for a Cardinals game, now stand anxious for pantry staples, hoping against hope that the food doesn't run out before the line does.

While the proud needy continue to sink deeper into the jaws of uncertainty, Republican elected officials remain numb to their pain. These officials' only real interests are power and further enrichment for themselves and their president; a president who continues to display unscrupulous behavior while committing crimes in plain sight. The Republicans seem to be more concerned with financing the new FBI building in Washington, DC, that Trump insisted must be **included in the stimulus bill** than with the number of school children going without three square meals. They seem more concerned with **passing the Qualified Immunity Act**, which will almost guarantee protection from prosecution when law enforcement officials break the law, than with assuring that American cities can pay their first responders and teachers. The Qualified Immunity Act has been widely criticized for emboldening police departments and the officers who would violate the civil rights of American citizens with acts up to and including the murder of black and brown people. It's very clear that this legislation aligns more clearly with the President's priorities than help for our heroes, our children, or our poor.

Another sticking point with the stimulus bill is that the Republicans are now demanding fiscal responsibility. Which is not ordinarily a bad thing, but why wasn't it an issue before billions of tax dollars got shoved into the bank accounts of their cronies in the first package? On Wednesday, March 25, 2020, the Senate passed a $2 trillion dollar relief package that was intended to help families, small businesses, and essential workers who were hit the hardest by the pandemic. Unfortunately, a host of undeserving corporations filed for this money, and got it. Millions of needy families still suffer because of the intentionally reckless behavior of the political leaders responsible for the distribution of those funds.

Steve Mnuchin, the US secretary of the treasury, formerly a hedge fund manager and investor, was chosen by Trump to oversee the distribution of this enormous sum of money. This task was completed without a system of checks and balances in place to ensure accountability for this money ever reaching the intended recipients.

I would like to think most Democratic leaders would be dogged and tireless in the fight for what is best for the spirit and soul of the American people. Now is **not** the time to be frugal at the expense of millions of Americans. Now is the time for our Democratic elected officials to stand and do what they were elected to do.

By the time this book is published, a decision as to what will be included in the next stimulus package will likely have been reached and the checks mailed. Hopefully, Chuck Schumer, the Democratic senate minority leader, and Nancy Pelosi, the Democratic house majority leader, will not bow to pressure and agree to a bad deal. They must realize that the future of millions have been entrusted to them and as such, stand strong and demand unfiltered support for those who put them there.

DISTINQUISHING THE TRUTH IS NOT AN OPTION

It doesn't matter to which political party we pledge our allegiance; the world as we know it has been hit by forces that demand that we adapt. The arrogance and unwillingness of our elected officials to recognize or care about the plight of the earth has allowed confusion and corporate interest to reign instead of unity and responsible leadership in a time of crisis and uncertainty.

Our world is facing the possibility of

destruction that will affect every facet of life. The sources of our destruction are both numerous and complex.

1. We struggle with systemic racism, which has initiated months of worldwide protest from those who have felt the weight of a knee on their neck, and the allies who support them.

2. An economic catastrophe only now in its infancy may ultimately topple powerhouses in the world of finance. The tentacles of this destruction will be far reaching and inescapable even for unsuspecting hoarders of wealth.

3. Natural disasters such as the fires occurring in the western states and the hurricanes along our southern shore will only intensify and usher in tornadoes and more severe weather events, displacing millions of people. All the while, this administration continues to deny climate science.

4. We are forced to confront the devastating effects of a novel Coronavirus, with all the physical, mental and economic trauma that entails.

Not Perfectly Divided

As of July, 2020, the number of Covid-19 cases worldwide stood at 19 million with over 700,000 deaths. The numbers are astronomical, but even more unbelievable is the fact that more than 160,000 of these deaths are owned by the US. That's more than 22% of the total deaths from COVID-19 in the world thus far. Stop, take a deep breath, and fully absorb that the wealthy, technologically advantaged US overwhelmingly accounts for a disproportionate number of deaths compared to the rest of the industrialized world.

We are the self-proclaimed leaders of the world in democracy, technology, research, and wealth. Yet, we lag far behind the rest of the world in our ability to formulate a plan to curtail the loss of life. This administration has not even established a unified message to promote the use of face masks even though masks have been proven to help stop the spread of the virus.

This administration, led by Trump, has fought against the advice of Dr. Anthony Fauci and Deborah Birx, esteemed physicians heading our coronavirus response. Dr. Fauci is a world-renowned immunologist and Dr. Birx has decades of experience in disease control and was a major player in the fight against the AIDS epidemic. Her loyalty to this country and her brilliance in this field has afforded her the respect of her peers.

Due to this administration's refusal to accept the advice of these respected specialists and other leading experts, thousands of Americans have died needlessly. To jump start the economy by putting people back to work, Trump has repeatedly ignored the recommendations of his leading scientists and physicians. His focus is clearly getting re-elected, and he believes a strong economy will ensure that.

Once again, his self-interest has caused the president to negate the welfare of the American people. It is obvious to me that the oath he took at his inauguration, to serve as a protector for all the people of this country, was meant to be disregarded at will.

Trump's brutish approach to almost every situation he encounters, coupled with his made-for-tv showmanship has been captivating enough to hold the undying attention of his partisan base. There's no other way to explain this mystifying degree of fanatical support he continues to garner, despite his obvious disdain for anyone who is not himself or enamored with his every tweet, no matter how ridiculous.

Republican Senators have shown themselves to be celebrated yes-men for this corrupt narcissist who constantly depreciates their value. These GOP Congressmen and women have violated *their* oath as well. They were sworn to protect the country from all threats, foreign and domestic, yet they tolerate confirmed criminal assaults against our soldiers and attacks on our elections in deference to Trump and his loyalty to autocratic strongmen.

United States intelligence agencies reported to the Trump Administration that Russian President Vladimir Putin paid Afghani soldiers to kill Americans serving in Afghanistan. However, Trump has repeatedly claimed these reports were not true, while also claiming he **never** received them! Proof once again that he lied to the American people for his comrade in the Kremlin.

The Republicans' determination to double down on their defense of the President's inactions are a self-serving attempt to curry favor with his base. The president's party supports him unfailingly, while the family and friends of American soldiers no longer trust the government to protect and defend their loved ones. We know that for some families, those fears have become the nightmare reality of a flag-draped coffin. We must understand that the enemies that fired shots at our soldiers did not act alone. Their accomplices sat in Washington, DC, and made no effort to aid in the safe return of soldiers who did not have to die. Their pursuit for re-election, however, continues.

GOVERNMENT DECISIONS CAN BE DEADLY AND LASTING

I am grateful that my childhood was, for the most part, filled with fond memories and fun times. Many of those memories involve my brother Joe, who was eight years older than me. He was strong and lovable. He loved sports and so did I. As far back as I can remember, Joe took me everywhere he went, and I enjoyed every moment. I would always wait for him to call out to me when he was about to leave the house. Our parents never objected to my going because they knew I was in good hands.

Joe would ask, "Fred, you wanna go with me?"

"Yeah, I'm ready."

"Well, let's go. Bring your baseball glove,"

"Okay," I would quickly reply grinning.

This dialogue happened often, but it never got old. He would take me to Lafayette Park close to our house. He would bring the bat and ball for the day's entertainment. Sometimes we would be in the park for hours playing catch, or he would hit ground balls to me to teach me how to field. I loved every minute of it!

We had lots of fun together and I was always riding high whenever we were together. Joe had one rule that I never forgot. He would look me in the eye as if he was looking right through me and say, "Fred, don't ever tell nobody what I do when we're together. Do you understand what I'm saying?"

"I understand."

Joe was a smooth talker and liked the girls at an early age, so he taught me way more than

Not Perfectly Divided

how to play ball. I followed his "no talk" instructions so righteously, that some people didn't know I could speak! I didn't want to do anything to destroy our time together.

I fondly recall times when Joe and I would go places and he would tell me to stay close. He would grip my head with his big, heavy hands and turn me in the direction he wanted me to go. If I started to drift a little, he would apply more pressure and I would get back on course. At times, he would apply too much pressure and I would let him know with a big yelp. "That hurt!" He would say, "Well go where I tell you!" I would just say, "Okay."

As I got older, I understood everything he did with me and for me was out of love. He was determined to keep me on track and out of trouble.

I was still pretty young when Joe graduated from high school and left for college. Shortly after he got to college, he was drafted into the army. At the time, the United States was at war with Vietnam and the death toll was rising daily. Joe went to Fort Leonard Wood in Missouri for basic training and preparation for war.

At the end of his six-month training, Joe got his orders, and it was not good. He was being sent straight to Vietnam. Before leaving, he was given a short furlough to come home and spend time with his family. When he got home, I noticed a change in him, but he never said anything to cause me to be concerned.

Joe was a peaceful and loving young man. He didn't want to go to Vietnam. He was not a killer. Which is why Joe decided not to report back to post after his furlough. Instead, he went AWOL—absent without leave. His attempt to avoid going to Nam was short lived. Three weeks later he was captured by military police and taken back to training camp. Next stop, Vietnam.

While Joe was AWOL, the platoon he trained with had left. When he arrived in Nam, his first priority was to find the guys he trained with at Fort Leonard Wood. Shortly after arriving, he ran into someone who gave him the news. His entire platoon had been killed moments after arriving. Joe was devastated, confused and shocked. By going AWOL, his life had been spared.

A few months later, my father informed me that Joe had been shot. At the time, my father didn't know how serious it was, but my dad assured me that he would find out. Shortly afterward, he told me Joe had been shot in the foot and was coming home. I never thought I could be so happy for someone I loved to get shot in the foot! I was relieved and so was my mother. But she was not going to be satisfied until she could see him and hold him for herself.

I will never forget the day Joe came home. My father was at work, so my mom wanted me to ride to the airport with her to pick him up. I was

Not Perfectly Divided

thrilled. This was a great day for us—to finally have my brother home again. Our mother was about church all the way to the bone. She was a devout Christian, and she prayed her way through all of life's difficulties. The ride to the airport was no different. She prayed as she firmly clutched the steering wheel. I looked on, hoping she would soon be relieved of her anxiety.

I had never heard my mother curse, and others did not curse in her presence. Her driving reflected her Christian demeaner. My mother drove a little pink Rambler and she always drove very cautiously (very slowly). She was not a good driver, but this day we arrived at the airport in record time. I could not believe how fast she had driven! In no time, we were pulling up to the passenger pick up area where immediately I spotted Joe.

"There he is!"

"Where?" Mom asked as she pulled to the curb.

"Right there! Just stop here," I told her.

I knew the exact moment Mom saw Joe. I heard her shout several times, "Thank you Jesus, thank you Jesus!" As we looked at Joe standing on the sidewalk, he seemed lost, as if he didn't see us. I knew something was wrong with him. I could see it in his eyes, but I quickly jumped out of the car anyway.

"Hey Bro," I said as I reached out my arms

expecting a hug. The hug never came. Joe looked at me as though I was an alien. I didn't say anything else to him, I simply pulled his bag from his grip and threw it in the trunk of the car.

Joe sat in the front with Mom while I jumped in back, still watching him closely. Mom grabbed him around his neck with a hug so tight I thought she might choke him.

"Thank you, Jesus!" She shouted.

Joe slowly raised his hands towards her arms, as if to disconnect from her grip. Mom was so happy to have him back. Other than the cast on his leg, I don't think Mom noticed anything strange about him. However, it would not take long for us both to know that this was not the same Joe we once knew.

Mom slowly pulled off and we were on our way home. She began asking Joe questions about his health as he sat stoically looking out the window as we traveled down Highway 70. Suddenly, out of nowhere ...

"F——k these motherf——kers," he shouted.

"Joseph!" Mom said, "What's wrong with you?"

He didn't say another word as we continued home. Neither did we. It was quiet the rest of the way. I cannot find the words to express how I felt that day. I couldn't believe how the fragile excitement of our reunion had crumbled. Joe was not Joe. Our Joe was gone, but at least he was

alive.
Years later, Joe told me after he learned his platoon had been massacred, that he went into survival mode. His singular hope was to make it back home safely.

According to *Britannica Beyond*, there were more than 3 million lives lost in the so-called Vietnam "conflict". Not a war, but a conflict is how our government officials described it then.

It is impossible to calculate the loss derived from the senseless and determined efforts of our government to force our democracy on a nation of people who rejected us and what we stood for. How do you quantify the grief of the millions of families who lost loved ones? How do you calculate those wounded, both physically and mentally? If you could calculate the actual cost, you would have to agree that the conflict was not worth the toll.

Although the US has not in recent decades experienced the massive losses of a Vietnam war, our soldiers are still dying in foreign lands on a regular basis.

Families are still made to needlessly suffer the loss of their young patriots who willingly serve to protect their nation's interest, wherever they are sent. Our government has often failed to support them adequately when they return home. No failure is so great as the Trump administration's refusal to even mention the murders of the soldiers killed in Afghanistan at the hands of Vladimir Putin.

The sanctity of our nation's heart, soul and spirit has been defiled, our soldiers placed in great peril under this administration. We must realize that the fight to regain our bearings begins with defeating Donald Trump.

We have an opportunity in November to make our voices heard. Regardless of who Joe Biden selects as his running mate, it is imperative that we VOTE. We cannot be swayed by voter suppression tactics or foreign influence campaigns.

If Biden is elected as the forty-sixth President of the United States of America, we must hold him and his administration accountable. His promise to select a woman as his running mate would be a great achievement in and of itself. However, we cannot rest on our laurels and become complacent.

Our goals for real and necessary change in the political arena must remain at the forefront of our agenda. The continued pursuit of justice and equality must be fulfilled. The following are a list of mandatory changes we need to achieve in the next four years.

1. Curb election spending. We must cap political contributions at every level of government if we are to achieve true and honest representation.

2. Reform our presidential elections. The Electoral College must be eliminated to allow for a true democracy with respect for the will of the people.
3. Institute police reforms. We must adopt a national police review model that incorporates citizens' review boards. The police should no longer be allowed to police themselves.
4. Eliminate qualified immunity. No one should be above the law, especially those employed to enforce it.
5. Enshrine healthcare as a right. Quality healthcare should be guaranteed for all Americans, as it is in every other advanced nation. A responsible plan would save taxpayers money in the long run.
6. Reign in medicine for profit. Prescription drug costs must be brought under control. Americans shouldn't have to choose whether to buy food or insulin.
7. Make wealthy people patriotic again. Loopholes must be closed to ensure everyone pays their fair share of taxes.
8. Save the Earth. We MUST protect the environment. Failure will be costly and increasingly deadly for future generations.
9. Preserve freedom of religion. No one should be persecuted or held at a disadvantage because of their religious beliefs, or lack

thereof.
10. Protect LGBTQ rights. No one should be discriminated against because of who they love, marry or identify as.
11. End the school-to-prison pipeline. Criminal justice reform is a must. The current system has become the latest strategy in a centuries-long attempt at genocide and legalized slavery.
12. Honor the nation's immigrant roots. We must reform the current immigration system that incentivizes business to seek cheap labor while punishing the poor non-citizen for answering the call. Citizenship should not only be for those who can afford it or those who come from "desired" countries with advance degrees.

This list represents issues I feel are the most urgent. We cannot be timid in our pursuit of matters of importance to the American people. We may not get what we ask for, but we must ask. In the words of my brother Harry, "a closed mouth won't get fed." No matter how homespun that adage, it holds true. We must speak up for the change we want and hold our elected officials accountable.

GANGSTER IN THE WHITE HOUSE SURROUNDED BY HIS HITMEN

Once disguised acts of aggression have been unmasked and emboldened in this country over the last four years. The current atmosphere has promoted open acceptance of wrongdoing by this country's political leaders. Shamefully, their dereliction of duty is of no consequence to them, as they operate out of sheer self-interest.

History, if we will heed it, can prevent us from repeating the tragic past. J. Edgar Hoover led the FBI from 1924 to 1972. During his tenure, there were eight presidents elected and eighteen attorneys general appointed to office. Hoover transformed the FBI into a professional and effective investigative force, then gradually began to use the agency's powers against those seen as political subversives. Given the Bureau's effectiveness and sophistication, Hoover soon found himself in possession of secrets from adversaries and allies alike. This gave him a stranglehold on the political arena and virtual omnipotence in Washington that was not easily undone.

Hoover's weapons of choice were intimidation and slander. He unleashed vicious attacks against the Black Panther Party, the Nation of Islam, Malcolm X, Dr. Martin Luther King Jr., and others who fought for justice and equality. His widespread misuse of power was used at will against anyone who got in his way.

The above-mentioned abuse of power should sound an alarm. Donald J. Trump, president of the United States of America, has been described as the most powerful man in the world. Despite the immense power he already wields, William Barr, the United States attorney general, appears to be serving as Trump's personal political hit man. Barr has proven his loyalty to Trump each time a challenge presents itself.

Agencies that fall under Barr's supervision include the Department of Justice, the Federal Bureau of Investigation, the Drug Enforcement Administration, the Bureau of Alcohol, Tobacco, Firearms and Explosives, the Bureau of Prisons, and the Office of Justice Programs.

With William Barr's enormous power and Trump's diabolical instincts, we could witness the dismantling of our democracy in a matter of years. Although not perfect, there is still great potential in our little republic, but we must realize she is neither too young, nor too old to fail. Now is the time for us to speak up and stand up for our democracy. In the words of the late Rep. John Lewis, we must be prepared to get into "good trouble."

Not Perfectly Divided

CHAPTER VI
GENDER DIVIDE

UNDERSTANDING STRENGTH AND WEAKNESSES

Perception is not reality unless a person allows perception to define them. The roles we take on in life have often been predetermined by society on the basis of gender, which can be misleading and counterproductive. The concept of gender roles stems from our early attempts to make sense of the biological differences between men and women in a social context.

Some would argue that the natural order of life dictates that certain responsibilities align with one's gender. Humans require a longer period of nurturing as infants than any other species. Traditionally, mothers were charged with the responsibility of raising the children while the fathers went to work. Over time, these roles have changed with the expectation of shared responsibilities.

Since fathers were traditionally expected to support a family, jobs in the dominant culture were almost exclusively the domain of men, and wages were set at levels intended to support their families. Women were viewed as caregivers, so fewer and lesser skilled jobs were open to them. Most that were available were low paying. Although Black women and other women of color always worked at substantially higher levels than White women, unfair labor laws made it hard if not impossible for women of any color to secure higher paying jobs.

In 1869, the National Women's Suffrage Association led by Susan B. Anthony and Elizabeth Cady Stanton was formed to push for an amendment to the US Constitution. The Women's Suffrage Movement led decades of fighting to win the right for women to vote in the United States.

It was a long, hard battle that lasted for almost a century, but the culmination of this struggle finally bore fruit. The Nineteenth Amendment was passed on June 4, 1919, and certified as law on August 26, 1920, granting women in the US the right to vote. However, the Nineteenth Amendment did not initially extend to women of African American, Hispanic American and American Indian heritage in all states because of widespread enduring inequality and racism, even from within the ranks of the women's suffrage movement. Although theoretically eligible to vote due to suffrage, it would take the passage of the Voting Rights Act half a century later, on August 6, 1965, for Black women to broadly exercise their right to vote.

Let's expand on the struggles women endured with the example of one all-time great freedom fighter, Ida Bell Wells-Barnett. Wells-Barnett was one of the founders of the National

Association for the Advancement of Colored People. She fought tirelessly to end lynching, prejudice, and violence. She also fought for equal rights for women, especially for Black women. Public lynchings were becoming a national pastime for whites in Wells's time. She campaigned against lynchings as a murderous intimidation tactic intent to keep Black Americans living more in fear of White rath than injustice.

Ida B. Wells and her sister soldier Harriet Tubman are some of the better-known activists to help pave the road to freedom, but that road didn't start or stop with them. Countless women worked tirelessly for the twin causes of racial equality and suffrage. Though their names were often forgotten to history, we owe them a tremendous debt of gratitude for helping to realize our more perfect union. Here are just a few of the names you should know.

1. Alice Paul (1885–1977): Paul was an American suffragist, feminist, and women's rights activist and one of the main leaders and strategists of the campaign for the Nineteenth Amendment. The amendment finally prohibited the states and federal government from denying the vote to citizens on the basis of gender.
2. Lucy Stone (1818–1893): Stone was a prominent US orator, abolitionist and

suffragist, and was a vocal advocate for women's rights. In 1847, Stone became the first woman from Massachusetts to earn a college degree.
3. Francis Ellen Watkins Harper (1825–1911): Harper was an abolitionist, suffragist, poet, teacher, public speaker, and writer. She was one of the first African American women to be published in the United States. Born free in Baltimore, Maryland, she had a long and prolific career, publishing her first book of poetry at the age of 20.
4. Mary Church Terrell (1863–1954): Terrell was one of the first African American women to earn a college degree and became known as a national activist for civil rights and suffrage. She taught in the Latin Department at the M Street School—the first African American public high school in the nation, based in Washington, DC.
5. Josephine St. Pierre Ruffin (1842–1924) was an African American publisher, journalist, civil rights leader, suffragist and editor of the *Woman's Era*, the first national newspaper published by and for African American women.
6. Shirley Anita Chisholm (1924–2005) Chisolm was an African American politician, educator and author. In 1968 she became the first black woman elected to the

United States Congress, representing New York's 12th Congressional District for seven terms from 1969 to 1983. She was also the first woman and African American to seek the nomination for president of the United States from one of the two major political parties. Her motto was *"unbossed and unbought."*

One chapter certainly could not hold all the acts of everyday heroism required of women to assert their financial and political freedoms. Neither could one book. This list would include the Black wives and mothers that sacrificed much to assure that they and their husbands and children would be able to hold their heads high and have a better opportunity at a more inclusive life. Chances are that your very own mothers, sisters and aunts are on that list somewhere. The foot soldiers aren't lionized by historians or celebrated by the culture. Theirs was the hard, unglamorous work in the quiet hours, sometimes with a baby on the hip. They were tireless in the pursuit of a better future for us. And here we are. May we never forget the intensity of the love that kept them marching forward.

THE HARDEST JOB: A MOTHER

My mother passed in 2007 at the age of 92, and I had the good fortune of being able to be with her in her twilight years. This was unmistakably one of the most satisfying periods in my life. It was an honor to return the love, care and devotion to the woman who had given so generously to me. My heart bubbles over as I think about our times together when she needed me most.

Mom was sick the last two years of her life. As she got progressively worse, she was in and out of hospitals and rehab centers. Even in declining health, she remained witty, funny, loving and insightful. I treasured every minute of her loving spirit. We talked frequently, and at this time of her life I found myself at her bedside often, still soaking up wisdom. It's amazing when I think about it. Even at her weakest, she still did more for me than I was able to do for her.

I vividly recall a talk we had one day when I was doing my best to pull some stories from the depths of her declining memory.

"How are you feeling, Mom?" I asked as she lay in the bed that would be her last resting place.

"I'm fine, Fred," she slowly answered.

I then began to share my day's activities with her because she loved to hear about my work. I bought houses sold as is and rehabbed them to turn a profit. As a matter of fact, before she got sick, I would pick her up from time to time and ride her around with me so that we could pick out good houses to buy. Mom had an uncanny way of picking the best houses, regardless of their apparent condition. It was amazing, especially for someone who had never been in real estate.

"I got a lot done on that house today," I told her.

"That's good," she answered. "What did you do?"

"I put the ceramic tile down on the floor."

"Did you finish?" she asked.

"Nope, but I should be finished tomorrow."

"That's good," she softly answered.

"Yeah, I'll be glad to get this finished. This might be the last house that I do."

She perked up the moment I said it.

"Why? You seem to be doing pretty good with those houses, and you like doing it."

"I do, but it's getting to be more work than I want to do."

There was silence for about thirty seconds, then she gathered herself, cleared her throat and spoke clearer than I'd heard her speak for months.

"Frederick," she said, and I knew I'd better pay close attention when she used my name that way.

"There's three jobs that I wouldn't want."

"What's that?" I asked.

"I wouldn't want to be a president; I wouldn't want to be a preacher; and..."

She then paused, held my hand and looked at me with a look that let me know that she wanted to make sure that I heard her every word.

"And I wouldn't want to be a mother."

"What made you say that?"

"That president has a big job, trying to do what's right for everybody, even if it hurts him. That preacher, he's got to deal with a lot of people, too. You got to be God-sent to endure everything that all those people put on you, because you care so much.

"But now, Fred, here comes that mother, umm, umm," She moaned with a deliberate and passionate tone.

"Fred," she repeated, "That mother, has got to go through some stuff that nobody else can do. Oh, that mother." She moaned.

Mom then smiled at me and relaxed a little more than usual.

"Get me some water," she said.

I got the water in a hurry and held it to her mouth.

"No, give me the glass, I can hold it."

And she did! She took a few sips and handed me the glass back. I left shortly afterwards, but the words that she spoke so passionately, they traveled with me.

That talk with her stayed on my mind all day long and into the night. Through all the trials and tribulations that my siblings, my father, and I took her through, that was the first time that I ever recall her giving us even a hint of her struggles in life.

Mom only lived a few weeks after that talk. Every bit of the time we had together was treasured. The culmination of her life brought the whole family together in those final weeks. My cousin, Mary Davis, was raised with us as our sister. She and her kids and grandchildren were there on a regular basis. We connected over stories and shared memories of Mom's life.

We all knew that Mom didn't have long to live, and I for one wanted her to pass on to her final resting place. I just didn't want her to hurt any more.

As always, when I finished working for the day, I would go to the rehabilitation center to be with her and comfort her. This one evening, when I got there two good friends of mine, Barbara and Ernestine Scott, had left just moments before I arrived. As I walked down the hallway, headed towards her room, the nurses spoke to me as usual.

"She rested very well today, Fred," Mom's nurse informed me.

"That's good," I said, as I hurried on to her room.

"There were two ladies that just left from visiting your mom, and they prayed with her."

"Good," I said.

As I entered mom's room, her eyes quickly opened. She knew I was there. I hugged and kissed her, just like always, and I then sat in the chair next to the bed and held her hand. I could see that she was still fighting to stay alive, despite all the pain that she continued to suffer. She knew me better than anybody, so I know she was able to see the hurt I felt because of her pain.

"Fred," she called my name, "I don't mind hurting, because I got to suffer to make it in."

She was talking about making it to heaven. Tears, began to moisten the corners of my eyes, but I tried to hold back. I didn't want her to see me cry. I then gently caressed both of her hands and looked at her with a renewed understanding of what had made her hold on this long. I began to pray with her, and I assured her that we all would be okay, even without her on this plane.

She smiled as I prayed for her to leave us and go to her heavenly home. Mom squeezed my hands tightly and gave me a look as if she was thanking me for giving her permission to leave. After kissing her on the forehead, hugging her and giving her thanks for all that she did, I softly whispered, "I love you."

"I love you, too," she said as she slowly loosened her grip on my hand. Soon after, I left feeling more relieved than I had ever felt in my life. I knew that I would never see Mom alive again. She died in her sleep the following morning.

I will forever have a warm spot in my heart for all those whose acts of love and appreciation helped give my mother a smooth transition in her final days. Before Mom was transferred to the rehab center, she was at Barnes Hospital. While there she had a regular visitor that was quite unexpected.

Reverend Jeff Johnson Jr. from the Circle of Life Church in St. Louis, Missouri grew up with me in the old neighborhood. He was a little older than me. We all still called him by the nick name we had for him before he became a minister, Jabo. Mom never went to Jabo's church, but that didn't matter to him. He still wanted to comfort one of the neighborhood mothers in her time of need, and he did that with his prayers and his presence without being asked.

WOMEN SACRIFICED ALL THE WAY TO THE GRAVE

As evidenced by my own mother, women's lives are sometimes complicated. When we view the women in our lives through the lens of their accomplishments and the obstacles they've overcome, in retrospect they are often more spectacular than we originally imagined. Through loss and obstruction hidden from our view, they carried on with determination and selflessness, often without a word of complaint. We eagerly accept and just as easily forget that sacrifice. This betrayal happens to generation after generation of our mothers, who just keep on advancing the cause.

Women of all nationalities protested, marched, and sacrificed on every front to gain equal rights. Due to a break in women's solidarity, the rights of all women did not advance equally. As mentioned before, African American women didn't get to vote for almost five decades after white women gained their rights, and it didn't have to be that way. White women turned their backs on the African American women that fought alongside them for fear of upending their own cause.

Ida B. Wells was in Washington, D.C., in the spring of 1913 with thousands of other women for a parade spearheaded by one of the country's leading suffragists, Alice Paul. Wells was representing the Alpha Suffrage Club that she founded in Chicago two months before. At the rehearsal, she learned that the white organizers wanted Black women to march at the back of the parade so as not to upset Southern delegates.

"Either I go with you or not at all," said Wells, one of the founders of the National Association for the Advancement of Colored People. "I am not taking this stand because I personally wish for recognition. I am doing it for the future benefit of my whole race."

Wells's act of courage was viewed as insubordination and a step backward for the white suffragist cause. So much so that cartoonists pilloried the suffragists in editorial cartoons of the day.

The Wells incident served to harden the position of anti-suffragists against the women's movement. With the tragic and fateful sinking of the Titanic still fresh in the minds of most Americans, anti-suffragists published cartoons in newspapers depicting the women of the Titanic jumping over men to get to lifeboats. Equal rights were the last thing on the minds of those ladies on the Titanic, but the cartoons mocked the mere suggestion of equal rights.

There are two prevailing myths when it comes to women's suffrage and the Nineteenth Amendment. The first is that when the amendment became law in 1920, most if not all American women won the vote. The second is that no Black American women gained the vote that year. Since we're marking the amendment's centennial, it's time to replace both falsehoods with facts. Voting rights in America have always been under attack for certain groups of Americans.

On August 26, 1920, the US Secretary of State certified that the Nineteenth Amendment to the Constitution had been ratified by the required 36 states. It became the law of the land: *"The rights of citizens of the United States shall not be denied or abridged by any States or by any State on account of sex."*

The Nineteenth Amendment did not, however, guarantee any woman the vote. Instead, laws reserving the ballot for men became unconstitutional. Women would still have to navigate a maze of state laws based upon age, citizenship, residency, mental competence, and more, that might keep them from the polls. The women who showed up to register to vote in the fall of 1920 confronted many hurdles. Racism was the most significant among them. The nation in myriad ways continued to stomp on the hopes of voting rights for women of color.

Those that opposed equal access to the vote began taking more and more drastic measures to deter voting by African American men and women. Poll taxes and literacy tests kept many black men from casting their ballots, but the unchecked intimidation and threat of lynching sealed the deal.

Many Black women did manage to vote in 1920. Some had been exercising that right for several years in states like California, Illinois and New York, where women's suffrage became law before the Nineteenth Amendment was ratified. Even more registered and cast ballots after its passage.

The battles women fought 100 years ago for constitutional rights and the downfall of discriminatory Jim Crow laws in the South still echo in 2020 as American women continue to work against voter suppression and for full access to the polls. Attempts to discourage and suppress the vote of African American men and women have not lessened. In fact, voter suppression tactics have become more obvious and brazen.

As unbelievable as this may seem for this day and age, Donald J. Trump and his Republican cronies are using every tactic imaginable to suppress the vote by enacting laws and implanting partisan supporters in key positions.

The writing seems to be on the wall for the presidential election on November 3, 2020. Mail-in voting is under attack in a ferocious way because Trump believes his bid for re-election would be greatly enhanced if mail-in voting stopped in some key states. It's just another ruthless Republican scheme to attack the voting rights of the American people.

Following along with all of Trump's lawsuits and legal shenanigans may seem complicated, but his strategy is as clear as a bell. Let's not forget that the Republicans have control of the Senate and the Presidency, which enables his plan for litigation up to and including the Supreme Court to be executed in broad daylight.

Even the postal service has been used to disenfranchise voters. The United States Postmaster General is the chief executive officer of the United States Postal Service. The Postmaster General is responsible for managing and directing the day-to-day operations of the agency. The Postmaster is now appointed by nine "governors," themselves appointed by the president with the advice and consent of the Senate. The governors, along with the Postmaster

General and the Deputy Postmaster General, constitute the full Board of Governors of the United States Postal Service.

Billionaire Louis DeJoy, who made major contributions to the Trump campaign, was appointed Postmaster General during the Trump administration. He has no experience as an employee with the postal service. Within months of his appointment in May of 2020, he instituted sweeping changes that will make it more difficult for voters throughout the country to cast a ballot by mail. Many of the nation's familiar blue mailboxes have suddenly been removed, postal sorting equipment dismantled, and postal workers have revealed reductions in overtime hours enacted to affect the timely delivery of mail across the country. These brazen actions were enacted despite the fact that the US Postal Service is one of a very few federal agencies authorized by the Constitution to serve the public good.

Thirty-six states now require voters to show some form of identification at the polls before voting. In addition, Trump has promised a military presence at the polls to guard against "voter fraud". Sounds like intimidation to me. At a time like this, it's hard to deny that the nation seems headed toward greater dysfunction and less democracy. Because of this, African American men and women may have as much difficulty voting in 2020, as they did in 1920.

LGBTQ AND TRANS CITIZENS FEEL THE HEAT

This age-old struggle for voting rights, civil rights, human rights and just plain protection under the law from bodily harm and death due to hate was waged for all citizens, including LGBTQ people. Even if you are in total disagreement with their sexual preference or gender identity, we must realize that with the choice to discriminate against one, comes the acceptance of discrimination against all. Don't rest easy because the persecuted group doesn't include you for the moment. Fascists always eventually demand that more groups are added to the list of unwanted and unprotected people.

As students of history, we know where this is headed. Sooner or later, you or someone you love and respect will be on the list. In essence, whichever group you belong to that's being walled off from justice, my fight and your fight are one and the same. We must partner with all those who are denied equal justice and protection under the law. We need to actively work to demand full rights for all people, and to disavow those who would accept that certain groups are peeled off from justice, one at a time.

Since the day that President Trump took office, his administration has waged a non-stop war against the rights of LGBTQ people. We see this trend at work at the Department of Housing and Urban Development. Despite policies that previously protected transgender people from housing discrimination, Trump's HUD under the direction of Ben Carson has openly reversed equal protection rules in homeless shelters and other public housing services that are paid for with our federal tax dollars.

No federal law prevents a person from being fired or refused a job on the basis of sexual orientation. The nation's largest employer, the US military, openly discriminates against transgender people. Mothers and fathers still routinely lose child custody or visitation rights simply because they are gay or lesbian, and gay people are often still refused the opportunity to adopt.

These discriminatory practices are relevant in all segments of life for LGBTQ people: healthcare, education, labor, even personal safety—the fundamental right to walk the street unafraid. Our freedoms and liberties are at times taken for granted until they're disrupted. A shocking act of violence can shatter the illusion that we are free from other people's bigotry, callousness and disrespect, even if the law is ultimately on our side. It doesn't have to be an attack on our person. An attack on a loved one or even a stranger can bring that reality home, as we witnessed this summer as millions worldwide marched to protest the death of George Floyd and other marginalized people like Dominique "Rem'Mie" Fells, and Riah Milton, two transgender women murdered this past June.

As devastating as it must be to endure unjust mistreatment by others because of who you are or who you love, I'm certain the pain of living a lie to avoid a giant cloud of alienation must be even more unbearable.

I have two stepdaughters from a previous marriage, Telisa Morris and Kaya Morris. Kaya is gay and as a matter of fact, she married her wife, Franita Staten, four years ago. I was highly appreciative when she asked me to give her away. I had never been to the wedding of a same-sex couple, so I didn't know what to expect. But I know what I got, which was a feeling of pure joy and happiness the moment I saw how beautiful Kaya was in her long, white flowing bridal gown. The look of love they showed for one another was overwhelming and satisfying. A father can't ask for more than to see his daughter happy and living her life to the fullest in a way that brings her unlimited joy.

Kaya was sixteen when her mother Lisa and I met. Our connection was always friendly and warm, filled with respect and admiration for one another. Like any family, we endured trials together. Lisa and I eventually got a divorce, but Kaya and I grew closer and closer as time went by. Because of our trusting relationship over twenty-five years, she granted me the opportunity to ask her questions about her sexual preference. I came away with a much better understanding of LGBTQ issues in general, and my daughter in particular.

In their desire to share their love beyond themselves and their existing family, Kaya and Franita decided to have a child together. When I spoke to her, Kaya was almost nine months pregnant. Because of this and due to COVID-19, I asked my questions by phone.

It wasn't long after our conversation began that I realized that Kaya wanted to talk about this aspect of her life as much or more than me. She wanted to share her story. Once we finished with a little small talk, Kaya asked me, "What do you want to know?"

"How long have you been gay?" I asked.

"That's hard to say, but I know that when I was six years old there was a stronger appeal for other girls than boys. But I didn't understand it at the time."

"That young?" I asked.

"Yeah, but I'm not saying it was sexual, but it was an attraction that I felt even at that age."

"That doesn't sound like a learned behavior." I said.

"It wasn't. There's no way I could've learned that at that age. But I know what I felt."

"Kaya, when did you first have a relationship with a girl?"

"I didn't do anything with another woman until I was grown and married with three kids."

"It took that long?"

"It did, because I was living a life that others would approve of, and not what was right for me."

"Wow, that's a long time to live that way."

"Too long," she answered, "But I'm relieved now, and I don't care what others think—I'm happy with who I am today."

"How did you finally open up to who you knew you were, after all those years?"

"I talked to my husband about my feelings and, like most men, he saw this as an opportunity to have a threesome. So he was more than willing to aid me in my quest for the discovery of my sexual awakening with another woman."

"What happened?"

"We started going to gay bars, and this is where I met a woman that I was really attracted to."

"How did that work out?"

"It eventually had a lot to do with the demise of our marriage, along with other reasons, but I was happy with my big step to being me, and free, for the first time in my life. And I knew that my life would never be the same again."

I asked Kaya several more questions, but what touched me the most was her answer when asked about the opposition she faced from those close to her when she finally decided to come out of the closet. At that point, she really opened up.

Kaya expressed explicitly the deep hurt and alienation she felt for years because of the way her own family treated her. She was no longer invited to family dinners unless she came without her lady friend. On holidays and special occasions, Kaya's mom would have dinner at her home, separate from the family members that didn't want to be around Kaya. This helped some, but it just wasn't the same. Early on, this caused a lot of pain, especially when her close cousin stopped speaking to her.

"But I stayed the course for my life and happiness, and if they can't accept who I am, then that's their problem, not mine. I'm happy with who I am, and I'm happy with who I'm with. I'm getting tired Fred," she said, "But there's one more thing that I need to say."

"What is it, Kaya," I asked.

"I love my life, and I love Free." (That's her nickname for Franita, her wife).

"Get your rest Kaya, and by the way, I love you, just the way you are."

"I love you too," she said.

After we hung up, I thought about the joy that I could hear in her voice throughout our phone call. I was even more appreciative of those who have been fighting for their freedom as a couple. I left the conversation more committed to advancing freedom's cause for LGBTQ people.

Fred Easter

ANOTHER GLASS CEILING SHATTERED

Women continue to pass the baton of justice work through a long and winding race to freedom. Even though the Nineteenth Amendment was flawed, its inception did provide another fracture in a glass ceiling that continues to crack with continued work and diligence.

So often, those that sacrifice the most are the least rewarded. Even though this holds true for multitudes of African American mothers, these prideful moms never stop working to prepare their children for success in an unjust society. From the blood, sweat and tears of these women, come some of our biggest advances. A few of these difference-makers are household names, but most are not. Young African American men and women owe them a debt of gratitude that can only be repaid by picking up the baton. Here are a few more of their names.

1. Rosa Parks (1913–2005): Known as "the Mother of the Civil Rights Movement" because of her role in the Montgomery Bus Boycott, Parks lit a fuse for activism that still burns bright. In 1954 she refused to give her seat to a white man, setting the stage for the legal actions and protests that began to unravel segregationist policies.
2. Nannie Helen Burroughs (1879–1961): Burroughs, an educator, church leader and

suffrage supporter, devoted her life to empowering black women. She helped establish the **National Association of Colored Women** in 1896 and founded the National Training School for Women and Girls in 1909.
3. Ella Baker (1903–1986): Civil rights activist and freedom fighter Ella Baker played a key role in some of the most influential organizations of the time, including the **NAACP**, the **Southern Christian Leadership Conference**, and the **Student Nonviolent Coordinating Committee (SNCC)**. In 1964, **SNCC** helped create Freedom Summer, an effort to both focus national attention on Mississippi's racism and to register black voters. Baker and many of her contemporaries believed that voting was an essential key to freedom.
4. Angela Yvonne Davis (b. 1944) is an American political activist, philosopher, academic and author. Davis came of age in Birmingham, Alabama, at the height of segregationist violence. She had been friends with several girls killed in the Sixteenth Street Baptist Church bombing. Davis credits her parents for her activism and the vision to see beyond a world limited by racial hatred. As a teen she led interracial study groups raided by local police. As an

adult, she joined the Black Panthers and an all-Black branch of the Communist party where she was an early proponent of ending the prison industrial complex. Her own 18-month imprisonment in connection with a politically charged murder case would earn international attention until her acquittal in June 1972. She was twice nominated as the vice-presidential candidate for the Communist Party in the US. Her book *Women, Race, and Class* (1981) is a well-respected history of the women's liberation movement.

These women and countless others paved the way for Black women to occupy seats of power today; people like Cori Bush of St. Louis, who recently ousted Lacy Clay as the Democratic nominee for Missouri's 1st Congressional District. And of course, there was another glass ceiling shattered when Joe Biden, the Democratic 2020 nominee, selected Kamala Harris, an African American woman, as his vice-presidential running mate.

Harris's pick as Biden's running mate would never have been possible without the broad shoulders of the women who came before her. Their work readied the way for Kamala Devi Harris, born October 20, 1964.

Harris has served as the junior United States senator from California since 2017. Before her term as senator, Harris earned her undergraduate degree from Howard University and a law degree from the University of California, Hastings College of the Law. She began her career in the Alameda County District Attorney's Office.

In 2003, Harris became the District Attorney of the City and County of San Francisco. Among her achievements as District Attorney, Harris started a program that gives first-time drug offenders the chance to earn a high school diploma and find employment.

Having completed two terms as the District Attorney of San Francisco, Harris was elected the first African American and first woman to serve as California's Attorney General. In this role, she worked tirelessly to hold corporations accountable and protect the state's most vulnerable people.

Over the course of her nearly two terms in office, Harris won a $25 billion settlement for California homeowners hit by the foreclosure crisis, defended California's landmark climate change law, protected the affordable Care Act, helped win marriage equality for all Californians, and prosecuted transnational gangs that trafficked guns, drugs and human beings.

While in the Senate she has introduced and cosponsored legislation to raise wages for working people, reform our broken criminal justice system, make healthcare a right for all Americans, address the epidemic of substance abuse, support veterans and military families, and expand access to childcare for working parents.

That list of accomplishments for most people might come at the end of a glorious career in public service. But not for Harris. She is at a place along the road rarely traveled before. If elected as vice president, upon breaking the tape, I know she won't finish with a victory lap. Like all those before her, she'll just begin the next leg of this race to equality.

I don't want to get ahead of myself by outlining the fights she'll endure after she's elected as vice president, because we will likely have many roads to cross before that happens. Let's not be naïve about this upcoming battle for her and Biden. The fight for this presidency will be more vicious and treacherous than anything that the US has ever seen because of Donald Trump and the Trump Party. But I'm sure that Biden, Harris and their enthused supporters desperate for change, will be able to hold off the attacks and come out victorious in this election.

As vicious and conniving as Trump and his comrades have proven to be, my greatest concern is for the inevitable in-fighting that will surely come from other women and minorities. At every point in history there have been people willing to obstruct progress toward their own advancement.

Although I'm not surprised, I have already witnessed the divide over Kamala Harris on social media, and it's only just begun. Although my introduction to the world of social media is relatively recent, my understanding of its power is clear. These forums can elevate users to unbelievable heights and tumble that same person into the pits of earthly hell. The accusations and untruths about Kamala Harris on Facebook and other social media platforms, seemingly from other black and brown people and women, is deeply disturbing.

I've noticed continued postings about how she mistreated many of her own people in the courts while working as a DA in San Francisco, even though her job was to uphold the law. It's a shame that we hold our own people to a higher degree of scrutiny than we do anyone else, even those that have a long history of unconscionable behavior towards our very sanctity of life and liberty. Her place of birth is now being questioned, not only by Donald Trump, but also by some that pretend to be loyal defenders of justice, equality and freedom. As ridiculous as these self-imposed setbacks are, let's not forget that there were slaves that fought with the South in the Civil War, in opposition to their own freedom.

CHAPTER VII
THE POWER OF SPORTS IN POLITICS

A shared passion for competition—the thrill of victory and the agony of defeat—have long bound athletes and observers alike in a love of sport. In the 1936 Olympics, Jesse Owens was in Germany competing against Carl Ludwig "Luz" Long, an Olympian who was the very embodiment of the Nazi party. At that time, Long held the European record for the long jump. He and his country's leaders were expecting to win a Gold Medal in the upcoming Berlin Olympic Games.

Long would eventually fight with the German army against the Allies during World War II and meet his end after receiving fatal wounds during the Battle of St. Pietro in 1943. Before that would come to pass, Long would face a different enemy: the African American track star Jesse Owens, who was the antithesis of Hitler's White supremacist theories.

Owens would ultimately make history at the 1936 Berlin Olympics by winning four Gold Medals, breaking or tying nine Olympic records and setting three new world records. But Owens didn't win all those medals on his own. According to some anecdotes, he had some help in one of those events. That help came from a very unlikely source; the future German soldier, Long.

Owens was struggling with the long jump,

so the story goes. The 23-year-old athlete had always excelled at the event, but this time he fouled at his first two attempts in the qualifying round. Owens struggled to regain his composure. That's when Long, his competitor and the favorite to win the event, allegedly stepped in. Not to taunt or mock, but to give advice.

The technical advice that he gave Owens helped him qualify and go on to win the Gold Medal against Long, which angered the German leadership. Not only that, but Long was the first to congratulate Owens on his long jump victory.

Turns out Long wasn't just a competitor, he was a long-time admirer of the famed American athlete, and a lover of their mutual craft. It's a big world with plenty of ways to share the wealth. In business as in life, true professionals, even rivals, respect and help each other succeed. By doing so they improve their craft, further the success of their profession, build relationships, share in the rewards, and maybe even help the world become a better place.

Some historians have proposed that, had Long defeated Owens in that event, he wouldn't have been required to fight in the war that ultimately claimed his life. Instead, the story of Long's sportsmanship survives to inspire athletes of another era and is recounted by entrepreneurs and inspirational speakers like Gene Marks, author and founder of the Entrepreneur Leadership

Network.

Bill Russell was another sports figure whose reputation transcended his sport because of his tremendous talent and desire to win at basketball. His relationship with his coach, Red Auerbach, was one of respect and a shared dedication to excellence through hard work and unequaled preparation. Because of their desire to win, the Boston Celtics, for the first time in NBA history, named five black starters: Sam Jones, KC Jones, Willie Naulls, Satch Sanders, and Russell.

Russell's playing days with the Celtics were far from joyous and rewarding. In the midst of winning eleven championships for the city of Boston, he was still treated with contempt and disrespect. After he helped deliver six NBA championships in seven seasons, vandals broke into his home, defecated on the beds and walls, and destroyed many of his trophies. He was constantly called the N-word throughout his career.

The mistreatment of successful African American athletes was not new. In fact, it was entirely normal. Even so, African American athletes like Russell were willing to take a stand against systemic racism, even when their outspokenness brought the risk of damaged careers or physical harm. This was also true of Tommie Smith and John Carlos, track and field athletes who accepted their gold and bronze medals for the 200-meters at the 1968 Olympics in

Mexico City with a fist raised in a Black power salute. This stance was taken to shine a light on the grave injustices harshly imposed on African Americans back in the US.

Displays of courage did not come without a price. Activism often soured future opportunities for wealth and security for the athletes and their families for years to come. Open displays of hatred and death threats were all part of the severe repercussions for standing up for your rights.

We can never forget the sacrifice of the self-proclaimed greatest boxer of all time. Muhammed Ali gave up boxing at the height of his career because of his refusal to join the United States military and fight in a war, Vietnam, that he did not believe in. He had help from supporters that enabled him to eventually regain his career and re-emerge as a heavy weight champion. He would ultimately become a global icon in the fight for justice.

The takeaway of all these stories is that in order to win, sometimes we must think outside of the box, gather allies and brace for the worst. This philosophy was true years ago, and it still holds true today.

That history of sports activism culminated in 2020 as the NBA, WNBA, MLB, American Tennis Association, NFL, Major League Soccer and the National Hockey League declared solidarity with Black Lives Matter. Players temporarily suspended games, took a knee or in other ways acknowledged the movement after the shooting of Jacob Blake, a twenty-nine-year-old African American man shot and wounded by white police officers in Kenosha, Wisconsin, on August 23, 2020. Three of Blake's sons, ages three, five, and eight, sat in the back of his SUV, frightened and traumatized as they watched their father gunned down by police.

Blake was shot after attempting to break up a domestic dispute in Kenosha. At some point during this melee the police arrived and soon became intent on detaining Jacobs. The video captured by witnesses clearly shows Jacobs attempting to peacefully get into his car, unarmed. Police attempted to prevent his departure by grabbing his t-shirt and firing seven shots into his back at close range. Despite this attempted murder by the police, Jacobs survived.

Days later, Jacobs' father found that his son, now paralyzed from the waist down, had been shackled to his hospital bed at the ankles. When interviewed, the police defended the practice as normal procedure for a subject wanted for third degree sexual assault. The shackles remained until his lawyer posted bond.

I can't fully express the pride and appreciation I felt as I watched elite athletes from every sport boycott their games in opposition of this country's continued mistreatment of black and brown people. It moved me so much that I rallied my wife, called my brother and daughter, and stood at attention in solidarity and recognition of this incredible display of unity. This was history in the making. A game changer recognized and supported by athletes and sports fans all over the world. Yes!

The willingness of these financially successful young men and women to put their careers on the line for a cause bigger than themselves will leave a lasting impression on me and everyone else watching. The next generation of athlete activists, at home and in quarantine, will forever recall the day sports stood still for justice. What a powerful example. These kids will know how to find their power when the time comes.

This journey we're on to freedom has been long and winding, but something about this national moment feels fundamentally different. Could this be the tipping point when the doors of injustice and systemic racism are finally knocked down? Only if we continue to coordinate in a way that will allow everyone involved to perform their part. This unified front must include the young women and men of Black Lives Matter, religious leaders of all faiths including the Rev. Al Sharpton and his National Action Network, the Rev. William Barber II and his new Poor People's Campaign, Minister Louis Farrakhan of the Nation of Islam, and the members of the Moorish Science Temple of America. Sincere political figures, activists, sports figures, entrepreneurs and people of all faiths are compelled at this moment to be the church and be the change.

With the activation of a broad coalition of allies and a global audience, our leaders have a moral mandate to act. Now's the time to put boots on the ground to do the good and necessary work of freedom fighting. I do hope and pray that these latest sacrifices, of black bodies, of personal loss, of pandemic marches and peaceful protests, have created a momentum that won't just fade into the annals of history as another lost opportunity. I'm convinced that we can take a giant leap forward if we all stay the course.

It was impressive to learn that a small group of NBA players led by LeBron James, Chris Paul and others reached out to former President Barack Obama by phone. According to Shams Charania, sports reporter for the Athletic, Obama advised James, Paul and the other players that they should play and express what actions they wanted to see taken before their return.

Katie Hill, a spokeswoman for Obama, confirmed to the New York Times that they also discussed establishing a social committee to ensure that the players' and league's actions led to sustained, meaningful engagement on criminal justice and police reform.

After talking with Obama, Michael Jordan, chairman of the league's Labor Relations committee, and team owners, the players decided to return under three conditions. The league and the National Basketball Players Association, of which Paul is president and James a former vice president, jointly announced the initiatives:

1. A social justice coalition composed of players, coaches and league governors will focus on increased access to voting, civic engagement and police and criminal justice reform.
2. Teams that own and control their arenas will work with local officials to turn the buildings into voting centers for the November general election.
3. Public service ads will air during playoff games to increase engagement in elections and raise awareness of voter access and opportunity.

These demands couldn't be more timely given our need to get people to the polls during a massive attempt at disenfranchisement. After the election, coordinated efforts will need to maintain pressure on the powers that be to advance issues of economic reform.

CHAPTER VIII
DIVIDED FAMILIES

THE WEAKNESS CAUSED BY THE DIVIDE

My story of lost relatives is nothing new, especially for African American families. In fact, this was probably the case for millions of families torn asunder under difficult circumstances over the past several centuries. Due to repeated family disruptions, the normal trajectory we aspire to, where parents can give their children a better launch than the ones they inherited, is often more a tale of broken dreams than dreams come true.

In my view, centuries of disconnection have bred an innate culture of dysfunction for poor Black families. Each generation is burdened with the task of starting all over again, rebuilding wealth, property and opportunities. This process doesn't allow family wealth to grow and it erodes pride in our family institutions. This in part explains the lack of enthusiasm for patronizing our own businesses. That lack of an entrepreneurial tradition is responsible for the overwhelming levels of poverty in Black neighborhoods.

UNKNOWN CONNECTIONS

My brief journey into the world of Facebook and Twitter has delivered some eye-opening revelations. Since my last name is Easter, I always assumed that any other Easter I came across was a relative of mine. It was a fair assumption since our family name is unique in a sense; associated more with a holiday than with surnames.

My father, Julius "JC" Easter, was born on August 4, 1917. He was a great storyteller and I loved listening to him recite our family history. His recollection of our family origin was that his grandfather, James Sr., was born a slave in Mississippi, but his grandfather's desire for freedom never waned. As such, his grandpa's early years were spent working and saving for that glorious day when he would be able to purchase his freedom.

When the day finally came, legend has it that he and his wife immediately left the plantation, burned and buried their clothes, looked to the heavens staring directly into the face of God, and denounced their slave names forever. Still looking to the heavens, my great-grandfather proclaimed that his surname was from that day forward Easter—the day of the resurrection. The day Jesus rose from the dead. That's what he and Jesus had in common! He was now truly alive for the first time in his life.

Even though he and his wife were married before they were freed, they made a vow not to have any children born into this world under the ownership of a slave master. Their vow of celibacy now at an end, they started their family. From this union five children were born. Augustus (Gus),

Hill, James, Joe, and Mary. After growing up, Gus and Hill moved to Arkansas. It's not clear what happened to Mary, but Joe and his brother (my grandfather James) moved to St. Louis, Missouri. My grandpa was affectionately called Papa by all his kids and grandkids.

Papa died before I was born, but his presence in the family lingered. His persona was still family folklore that was the topic of conversation well into my teenage years. He was a wise man who earned his degree in Agriculture at Tuskegee Institute in Alabama. Soon after leaving Alabama he returned to Mississippi, where he eventually purchased some land and began farming. This worked out well for years, so he was ultimately able to purchase more land. This made him an uppity Negro in the eyes of some resentful Southern Whites. These ill feelings for Papa proved to be the beginning of the end for him and our family in Mississippi.

The Easter family's abrupt departure from Mississippi began one hot summer afternoon in 1922. On this day, my father JC and my uncle Luke were 5 and 6 years of age. Harry and Idamae, the two youngest, were playing with their older brother and sister, Robert and Minnie. Papa sat on the front porch, watching his kids play. The fun soon ended when two unexpected visitors rode up on a horse and buggy. Two White men, both sporting scraggily moustaches and beards with big brim cowboy hats, sidled up.

"Go in the house," Papa said.

Without any hesitation, Robert and Minnie quickly rounded the three younger kids together by their arms and rushed them into the house. Before Minnie closed the door behind them, JC heard one of the White men say loud and forcefully, "Now James, did you forget what I told you boy."

That was the last word he heard from outside because Minnie quickly rushed them all to the back room of the house, as far from earshot of the strangers and Papa as possible.

As far as JC knew, nothing else happened that day, but he knew without a doubt that the tension in the house for the next several days was so thick you could cut it with a knife. This feeling of uneasiness made it difficult for him to sleep and even more impossible when he heard Papa leave the house shortly after loading his hunting rifle. This became a nightly ritual until that chaotic night that finally displaced my family from Mississippi to St. Louis.

Even though he was only five at the time, bits and pieces of this frightful night were forever embedded in my father's memory. It was late night or early morning when Papa stormed into the house, shouting directives to Robert and Minnie to get the other kids ready to leave. It wasn't long before everyone was dressed and ready, still scrambling to gather precious items that weren't too heavy to carry. All the kids rushed out of the house. Minnie carried Harry, while Robert led the way. They headed toward the river, but immediately after fleeing the house JC turned around, only to see their house on fire. Soon thereafter, Papa caught up and led the way to the river.

To JC's surprise, there was a boat that he had never seen before sitting at the bank, and they all quickly got in. Once everyone was aboard, Papa quickly pushed it into the water and began to paddle at a rapid pace. He didn't slow up for what seemed like forever. The next thing JC knew, someone was shaking him awake as they all got off the boat.

They walked for what seemed like miles and miles through weeds and dirt roads, arriving at the house where their mother Maud was raised in Clarksdale, Mississippi. Maud died not long after giving birth to Harry. As a result, my father JC's memory of his mother was relatively vague. But Maud's sister Katherine Williams remembered him and greeted them with the royal treatment when they showed at her door that day.

Aunt Katherine had a daughter named Cora. Cora was older than JC and his brothers and sisters, and because of this she behaved like a little mother hen toward her younger cousins. This was especially true of JC because she had named him, which gave them an everlasting bond that filtered down to their children later in life. All the kids were loving every minute of their stay in Clarksdale, but this joy would not last long as Papa made the decision to leave for St. Louis where his brother, Joe, had moved years before.

FAMILY RESEARCH

James Easter and his wife Maud had seven children: JW, Robert, Minnie, Luke, Idamae, Harry and JC. JW Easter was my father's oldest sibling. He was born in 1899, ten years earlier than any of his other siblings. I never knew anything about him until I visited the African American History Museum in Washington, DC, in 2019.

While there I had a session in the Robert Frederick Smith Explore Your Family History Center Workstation. Within minutes after logging into their website, to my amazement, I discovered JW Easter, an uncle that I had never even heard of. Since then, I have questioned several family members about my discovery, but no one seemed to know anything about JW, other than Nana Easter, my cousin in Cleveland. Nana is my Uncle Luke's daughter. She remembered her dad saying he had an older brother named Joey that died young, but she didn't know how or when his death occurred.

Soon after James Easter and his family arrived in St. Louis, he met Annie White, and after a rather short courtship, they married. From this union two kids, Ruby and Wilbert, were born. Annie also had two kids from a previous marriage: Rozelle and Izelle. It was a perfect blended family for the kids as well. They all became very close and remained that way throughout their lives.

At this point my family research had a dual-purpose. I wanted to write a testament to the unjust disconnection of our families from our family home in Mississippi, and I hoped to find others through social media that may have a connection to our family story. I've befriended more Easters on Facebook and Twitter than I even knew existed in the last month or two. I'm sure some of us have a connection, and it would be nice to know about their stories, too.

MY MOTHER WAS BORN A WARD

As complicated as the lineage for my father's side of the family has proven to be, my mother's (the Wards), is much more hidden and confusing. During my visit to the African American History Museum in DC, I also researched my mother's family. I found no documentation of any family further back than my grandmother and her siblings. I do know that my great grandmother's name was Poly Ward, but I never heard her husband's name.

This was strange to me, especially since my grandmother, Francis Ward, had eight siblings. Not only that, but they all seemed to be very close except for the two that left the family at an early age, never to be heard from again. The six brothers and sisters that remained were, George, Jerry, Elizabeth, Arlena, Aunt Washee and Jenny. I was never told the name of the two that left, but George, Elizabeth, Jenny and Washee lived their lives out in the same place they were born and raised, in Hamburg, Arkansas. Jerry moved to California, while Arlena and my grandmother moved to St. Louis.

MEET ME IN ST. LOUIS

My Grandmother, Francis Ward, had one child, my mother Marie. Marie's father, based on the bits and pieces of information that I've been able to retrieve, was called Red and he worked on the railroad.

Marie had a wonderful childhood in Hamburg, Arkansas, even though she was the product of a single mom. She was truly raised by a village that consisted of aunts and uncles that adored her. In spite of the love and comfort she found in her small family, her ambition overrode all that was available to her in Hamburg. Soon after graduating high school, she moved to St. Louis with other family members to seek her fortune.

Upon her arrival in St. Louis in 1934 there were two things waiting for her—a job and a place of family worship at Rising Star Missionary

Baptist Church at 1709 S. Third St. She was a faithful member there, even after the church moved to 3424 Lasalle. She remained a member there until she died in 2007.

After a few years in St. Louis, working and going to school to be a nurse, Marie met JC Easter. Initially her aunts, uncles and cousins presumed that this attraction to JC would soon pass. But, their assumption proved wrong, and in 1940 they wed over the objections of almost every one of her relatives. Their objections didn't appear to be selfish or personal. They just wanted what they thought was best for Marie—and it wasn't JC. He was viewed as a worldly man and they desired a church man for her.

Church man he wasn't. But JC proved to be a good man that believed in God even though he didn't attend church. Even her minister, Reverend Sherman Glover, was against the marriage unless JC changed his ways and joined the church. Nonetheless, JC's resolve to maintain his lifestyle and Marie's determination to be with her man eventually prevailed. They were together for almost 67 years!

THE FAMILY

As Dad told it, Mom was the quintessential church girl, and she was having no parts of sex or anything sex-adjacent until after marriage. This was ultimately part of the allure that made her irresistible. As a result, nine months after their wedding day, my older brother Harry was born on January 15, 1941. My brothers Charles and Joe were born three and four years after Harry (respectively). I was born September 10, 1953. That's when Mom and Dad decided that they were satisfied at last. That last part of my tale has been disputed by my brothers, **but it's my story and I'm sticking to it!!!**

CAN THE FAMILY STAY TOGETHER?

We now live in a different cultural moment when parents talk more and share vital family information with their kids. It wasn't that way with most families I knew when I came up in the '50s and '60s. My family seemed to be even more secretive than most. I learned at an early age not to listen in on grown folks' conversations and butting in with some verbal input was totally out of the question. Had I done that once too often, I may not be here now to tell my story.

For the most part, my childhood was filled with joy and precious memories, even though my mom and dad both worked full time jobs to make ends meet. I was never at home alone because my grandmother lived with us. My mother and father brought her and Aunt Arlena to St. Louis after Harry was born. Aunt Arlena didn't live with us, but she was prominent in all my early childhood. Because of this I, too, had a village that raised me, like most other kids in the neighborhood. It was always a comfort to know that wide-spread neighborhood support was there, even though at times I yearned for less accountability.

There was one moment of inclusiveness in grown folk business that I regretted being a part of that would have a great effect on my life. It was the summer of 1963. I was outside playing in the street in front of the six-family flat that we lived in. My father pulled up in his new Pontiac and he was looking sharp. I wanted to be just like that man. He was good looking, and he always had an air about him that was pleasant, engaging and he was just fun to be with. But I wasn't ready for what I was about to hear.

"Freddy," he called out after getting out of the car.

"Can we go riding?" I asked. I had been waiting on him—I was overjoyed at the thought of riding with him in that new car.

"Not now," he answered. "Come on in the house, we need to talk."

"Okay."

I quickly caught up to him. At that point he put his hand on my shoulder and we walked in the house together. We went to the kitchen, my brothers Joe, Charles and my mother were already seated at the table. Dad motioned for me to take one of the seats, and I did. I knew at that moment, something serious was going on and I didn't know what to expect, but it was scary already.

I began looking around the table at the faces of my family, trying to see something in their eyes that would give away what was going on. I didn't have to wait long. My father began with a shocking blow.

"Your mom and I are breaking up. We're getting a divorce," he said,

"What does that mean?" I asked,

"Well, Fred, that means I won't be living here anymore."

I knew what it meant, but I didn't want to hear what I was hearing. I was stunned. Speechless. It was as if all sound stopped. I couldn't hear a thing my dad said after that. I could only see his mouth moving. It wasn't long before I heard Joe say,

"I'm staying with Mom," and Charles soon repeated the same words.

"What about you Fred," My Dad asked,

"What about me what?"

"Do you want to be with me or your mom?"

"I want to be with you," I answered.

Just that fast I saw visions of no more stern rules from Momma and Grandmamma. I would be able to do whatever I wanted to do because Dad was not the rules enforcer. I would soon be free. That vision of uninterrupted freedom didn't last long.

"You're staying with your mom," Dad

quickly replied. I didn't understand why he asked me when he knew the decision had already been made.

Although my dad was still there at least once a week, it wasn't the same. That was the longest year of my life. Not only that, but I'd never seen my mom so sad, even though she did all she could to hide the pain.

My mom and I talked more during that time than ever before, but she never said one negative thing about Dad. She wasn't made that way, and neither was he. They really loved each other, but they were both unyielding in their desire to live life exactly the way they wanted.

Mom was strictly about family, God, work and church. Dad was dedicated to work family and partying. Not only that, but I later found out that his inability to partake in his preferred pastimes of drinking and smoking weed at home finally proved to be more than he could handle. Those are the perils of loving someone that you have nothing in common with.

THE MOVE AND THE RECONNECTION

It was the summer of 1964, a little more than a year since the family separation. I was in Grandmomma's room, talking with her. She loved it when I slowed down long enough to share some of my day's activities with her. She dedicated her life to us. I don't think she had another man in her life after my mom was born, but that was fine with me. I was her favorite. We had a connection like no other. I didn't even mind her dipping snuff and spitting it into the can she kept close by. I was just glad that she never asked me to empty that can. I might have disobeyed a direct order had she ever asked but she was loving enough to keep that to herself.

"Why aren't you ready to go?" Granny asked.

"Go where? I didn't know we were going anywhere," I said.

"Go get dressed, and hurry up," she said.

It wasn't long before Granny, Mom and I were ready. We got into the car, going somewhere that I knew nothing about. I realized this because we were passing places that I'd never seen before. It was as though the longer we rode the nicer the scenery became. I asked once or twice about our destination, but as a result of their silence on this subject I gave up and just looked at all the unfamiliar houses and streets. Fair Grounds Park was beautiful, not to mention how big it was. I was still looking out the window when the car came to a stop in front of some of the most beautiful houses that I had ever seen.

"Let's go in," Mom said.

I couldn't ask any questions because I was too busy admiring the well-kept yards with bright green grass in front of all the houses. Another thing that struck me was that all these houses either had one or two doors instead of four, six or eight, which I was accustomed to. Granny and I followed Mom into this pretty house that had two doors. Upon entering, I noticed that there was no furniture, but the beauty of the hardwood floors and pretty white walls were things that I'd never seen before. But the best sight of all had nothing to do with house. It was the sight of my dad coming into view from another room.

"Hey man, how are you doing." He casually asked, as he flashed that big, beautiful smile. My face lit up with overwhelming joy from the sight of him.

"I'm doing fine," I said.
"How do you like it?"
"Like what?"
"The house."
"It's nice. Why," I asked.
"Because this is our house, this is where we'll be living." I didn't show my excitement, even though I was bubbling over with joy.

"What do you mean 'we'? Will you be here too?"

"Yeah, man, we'll all be living here together."

My dad then placed both of his big hands on each one of my shoulders and looked me in the eye.

"I'll never leave you again. As a matter of

fact, your mom and I are getting married, and I want you to give her away. Will you do that for me?" he asked.

"You know I will! When will the wedding be?" I asked.

"In a few minutes. I'll let you know when we're ready, okay?"

I could only nod my head in agreement, as I was too busy looking at the joy in the faces of my mom and grandmomma. This was the happiest day of my life! I had prayed, over and over again for Daddy to come back home, from the moment that he left. This was a dream come true! Not only that, but a new house, too! I was floating on a cloud; on a high that was immeasurable. I wasn't going to pinch myself. I decided if this *was* a dream, I didn't want to wake up.

"Go ahead man, look around the house and check out the backyard. I'll be in here talking with your Momma."

I quickly began moving around the house, looking at every room. This house was beautiful and bigger than I thought. There were six rooms and a basement with ceilings tall enough for grown folks to walk around comfortably. The back yard was nice and big, with green grass just like in the front. But the most amazing thing, the thing that I couldn't believe, was that there was a house for the car. I later found out that this was called a garage, but whatever the name, it was special!

THE MARRIAGE

"Fred! Freddy!" My dad shouted. I was still out back, but I had left the yard and I was now in the alley talking to some other kids that lived right down the street.

"Yeah, Dad, what is it," I shouted back.

"Come here,"

"Okay, I'm on my way." After letting my newfound friends know that I would see them later, I ran to the house. My dad stopped me as soon as I came through the door.

"Slow down, man," He said as he held me by the arm. "Let's straighten your shirt so that you'll be looking right for the wedding."

"Ok," I said,

"What about me, how do I look?" he asked.

"You look good, but you'll look even better next to Mom."

He smiled, showing great appreciation from the truth in the words I had spoken. He was happy. It was written all over his face. At that moment, I heard Momma calling me.

"Come here, Frederick,"

"Okay, here I come. Where are you?" The house was so big that I had to navigate my way around the rooms to locate her.

"I'm here, in the back bedroom. Just come on in," she said.

I followed her voice and it wasn't long before I pushed the door open and there she stood, as pretty as ever. She wasn't wearing anything too fancy. She was dressed in a long, pink dress with a flower attached to it that made her glow.

"How do I look?" she asked.

"Momma, you're beautiful!"

And she was. Even though I'd seen her in that dress before at church service, she wasn't as beautiful then as she was at this moment.

"What do you want me to do?"

My grandmother answered for her, as she picked and pulled on the dress, to give it just the right effect in each place. All this time Mom was gleaming with joy and Granny was working feverishly to assure herself that everything was right. Occasionally she would step back, peering over the top of her glasses to get an eagle's eye view of her daughter. I could see the pride in Granny as she slowly leaned back, smiled and gave a short nod of her head showing her approval. I think her satisfaction was as much about her work on the dress as it was about how good Mom looked. Either way, we were all happy and ready to do our part.

"Okay Frederick, when they call for me to come in, you're going to take me by the arm and walk me to the front room. You will then keep walking until we are face to face with your dad. At that point you will give my hand to him and you can then walk away. Can you handle this?" she asked.

"Come on, Mom, you know I got you."

Moments after mom gave me strict instructions on what my every move would be, there came a knock on the door.

"Come in," Mom said.

Uncle Robert then opened the door and quietly whispered, "We're ready."

"Okay, Uncle," I spoke up. "We're on our way. Okay Mom, let's go."

I gently took her arm, and we started our march towards the door. Like life out of the movies, the door swung open and we hit our stride on our walk of love. I was proud, happy and with every step I took I could feel my chest swelling. I felt ten feet tall, even though I was short and small. We finally reached my dad, and he extended his hands as I relinquished mine so he could take it from there.

All six of the other people at the wedding, Uncle Robert, (Ree) his wife, Aunt Sister, Granny, the wedding couple, and Reverend Andrew Smith who performed the ceremony, seemed to have gotten a big kick out of my performance. I listened to the vows intently and it wasn't long before the preacher gave dad permission to kiss the bride.

They kissed and that was it. We all mingled for a few minutes. I took a moment to observe Mom and Dad as they talked, and I was almost satisfied. But I still had one other question for them, and I asked as soon as I got them together alone. "Did we get some money that I don't know about."

They both looked at me kind of puzzled.

"What do you mean, man?" Dad asked,

"How did we get this house?"

Dad laughed and Mom smiled.

"Hard work, Fred, hard work."

And then Mom spoke, "That's right, working hard together, that's what it took."

I was satisfied.

CHAPTER IX
FAMILY CHALLENGES

THE NORTHSIDE

It seemed we made a smooth transition to our new life at 4706 Lee Ave. Mom and Dad were doing fine. Dad would smoke his weed, but never in the presence of Mom, though he drank his alcohol openly. Just seeing us happy was all Granny wanted.

Joe was doing well, even though he was forced to leave McKinley High School and transfer to Sumner. He quickly found new friends, which he was good at doing. Charles wasn't there often. I think he was still living on the south side with a lady friend. He always was a lady's man. Harry was living on the south side with his lady, Willie Mae Anderson.

And me? I was having the time of my life. I went to Scullin School and I made lots of new friends. I had the occasional fight because I was tested just like any other new kid. I didn't care because I was accustomed to fighting from living on the south side. But once I got established, I was left alone and that was good for me.

I loved playing baseball, so I gravitated to all the ball players around my age. There were some good ones. Adolfus Chancellor, Bob Moore, Willie MaCambry, Larry Pruitt, Fred Hilliard, and Alois and Stanley Bolden to name a few. I also hit

Not Perfectly Divided

against a flame thrower named Roy Branch. That was a challenge, but I stood my ground and I even got a hit against him. There were many others, but those guys stand out because we played on the same teams or we were rivals. Those were fun times that I'll never forget.

In July of 1967 I had established myself as one of the better players on my baseball team. Because of this, I was chosen to play in the All-Star game. I was excited that this would be my first time playing under the lights in Fair Grounds Park. I couldn't wait. I told the entire family and some friends about the game with the hopes that they would show up to see me. It felt big-time in my world, and I was ready to have a good game so they could see my skills.

The position that I normally played was catcher, although I played many others. I was always willing to play any position as long as I could start. It was the end of the first inning, and I'd batted in the top of the first, hitting a double and stealing third. That was a good start, but I was looking forward to doing more damage to the opposing team. I headed out to center field to man that position, but soon after getting set, a strange thing happened.

Dad and my brother Joe were sitting in the stands watching the game. Periodically I would look their way. I then noticed Hoop, one of Joe's friends, walk over to where they were sitting. He never sat down, but they all left immediately without saying a word, or waving, or anything. I wanted so much for them to see me play the game, but there was nothing I could do. I finished playing the best I could, and we won easily. I had two more hits and two runs that qualified me for MVP. I didn't win it, but I *was* in the running.

After the game, the coaches took all the players to White Castle for hamburgers, fries, and a soda. We had a good time, eating and talking about the game. After that, the coach dropped me off at home. I noticed an unusual number of cars parked on our street, but I dismissed it as nothing important. I opened the door and stepped into a house that was packed with thirty or forty people, easily. My initial thoughts were that they were here to celebrate my big game. But it didn't take long for me to realize that something wasn't right. Just the look on their faces told me that.

All eyes were on me but those weren't looks of joy, but of pain. I was looking in their faces for answers, but what I saw was foreign to me. While I still stood close to the door, my dad walked up to me and said,

"Fred, come with me, I have something to tell you."

I didn't say a word, I simply followed him to their bedroom. Dad told me to close the door and that moment, my world changed.

"Your brother Charles got shot. He's dead,

Fred."

I stared into nothingness for how long? I don't know. Then, once again I heard my father's voice.

"Are you okay?" he asked. "He's dead and there's nothing we can do about it."

"What do you mean, there's nothing we can do about it?"

He didn't say a word, but at that very moment I could hear my brother Joe's voice through the door.

"I'm ready," Joe said.

I walked out to see exactly what he was ready for. The moment I saw his face, I knew he wanted revenge on whoever had done this to Charles, and so did I. Joe looked directly at me, but it was as if he couldn't see me. The moment Hoop called to Joe, "Let's go man," I knew what my next move would be.

I dropped my baseball glove on the floor, proceeded to the front porch, knowing that they couldn't leave without passing me by. In my mind, I was going too. It wasn't long before Joe and Hoop came out the door, and I could see the pistol in Hoops waistband.

"I'm going with you," I announced as if this was a certainty instead of a request.

"You ain't going nowhere," Joe quickly said, "Get your little ass back in the house."

"I told you, I'm going too."

"Let's go, Joe," Hoop said again.

Before another word was spoken, someone opened the door and said, "They just found Donnie, dead."

We all went back in the house, searching for answers. It was reported that Donnie Crumer shot and killed Charles, and immediately afterwards he went to Buder Playground. At that point, he shot and killed himself.

"How could he do this?" I asked myself. First, he kills my brother, then he denies me the satisfaction of getting revenge.

I was finished for the night. I went to Mom and Dad's room and fell asleep on the bed with my baseball uniform on. I didn't wake up until the next morning. The following days were hard for me. My friend that lived across the street, Steven Joiner, helped me immensely through this and I will forever be grateful to him for that. He came to the funeral, too, making sure that I saw his smiling face in the crowd.

It was packed in that church and I couldn't wait to get out of there. It finally ended, and not a moment too soon. In later years, I still tried to make sense of my brother being killed at twenty-two years of age, before his life had even really begun. The greatest tragedy in this is that Donnie, his brother Larry, and my brothers Charles and Joe all grew up together. They thought that they knew each other, but nothing could be further from the truth. Donnie had just returned home from Vietnam maybe a month or two prior to this tragic day. He and Charles got into an argument about what seemed to be some minor thing. Certainly, nothing worth killing or dying over. But I suppose damage done to him in Vietnam reached thousands of miles away and claimed two victims that were never counted as casualties of war. Not only that, but the family and friends of these men were at a loss as well. All because of a meaningless war that was still extracting a heavy price long after the conflict ended.

THE EIGHTH GRADE

Following this summer of grief, we were still looking for ways to heal our family's loss. Every now and then Mom would be talking to me and call me Charles. I never once corrected her, but I found out later that I wasn't the only one who experienced that. At times I felt a little lethargic, although I didn't know what to make of it.

I do know that I found great refuge at school with my classmates and my new teacher, Mrs. Mayo. This is one of the reasons that I feel so bad for kids today, that are not able to go to school because of this coronavirus. God only knows how many children need friendship or healing from the hardships at home, especially in a world that's much more complicated than it used to be once upon a time. I'm sure the loss of in-school learning will have ramifications for years to come.

It wasn't long after the eighth grade that my life began to come unraveled. I was in and out of juvenile detention, which eventually landed me in prison, not once, but five times in the next twenty-five years, and in three different states—Missouri, Illinois, and Colorado.

As smart as I thought I was, I often wondered how I could have chosen such a reckless path in life. Even after making sense of some of my foolishness, I *still* couldn't get on the right track due to my heroin addiction.

My desire to live a different life evaded me in the early years of my addiction. In fact, I thought I was living the best life possible, even though I was only successful at making drug dealers richer and enhancing the prison population of various states. But even more than those great failures, I disappointed my Granny, my Mom and Dad, not to mention all the others that for one reason or another put their trust in me. If breaking their hearts was not enough, my parents endured the same let down from my brothers Joe and Harry. We all chased heroin as if it were our own personal savior.

The most amazing thing about our drug addiction is that our parents never turned their backs on us. As a matter of fact, there was never a time that we didn't have a key to their home if we wanted one. I recall a talk between my dad and I, while I was down on my luck, living in their house, high at that very moment.

If you know anything about a deep-thinking drug user, you will know that there will be some moments of unfiltered truths and in depth-reasoning. I was no exception. This day, I sat in my parents' house, on their couch, watching their television and I was bothered by something that made no sense to me. My dad sat in the chair next to the couch where I was sitting. We were watching the ball game—or maybe I should say *he* was watching the game, because I was damn near too high to see anything. We all called our dad Jay, and we did so until the day that he died.

"Hey Jay, I want to ask you something."

"What is it Fred?" he asked.

"I don't understand you."

"What is it about me that you don't understand?"

"Well, I don't understand why you are still f g with me, while I'm not doing a damn thing to help you or myself. I just don't get it."

He grabbed the remote to the TV and turned it off, and looked at me sternly, so as not to be misunderstood. I was damn near sober at this point. He then said the words that I will never forget in my life, and he said it slowly and deliberately.

"It's because you are mine, I love you, and I

don't ever want to lose another son."

I didn't say another word, but I thought about it. I decided I wanted nothing to do with love. Love was too powerful. I would never let anyone do me the way I've done them. But little did I know that same love proved to be the motivating force that pulled me out of darkness and back into the light.

I know my daughter is going to kill me for telling her age, but I have got to tell my story. She can contest the accuracy of the dates, and I won't argue the point, but from my recollection, I was blessed in 1979 with an angel. The love I felt for her was greater than the love I felt for myself at that time. My transition from drugs wasn't immediate, but the process started the first day I laid eyes on her. This happened when she came out of the comfort and darkness of her mother's womb into the light of life.

She screamed and hollered as most newborns do at their debut. A feeling of mixed emotions came over me. I was happy but apprehensive about all the life changes I would need to make. I had never felt as needed by anyone as I did in that moment. Before I left the hospital that night, I sat in a room by myself and made a vow not to use drugs anymore. I was serious, but not nearly as serious as the addiction that gripped my body. I struggled for a day or so, but it wasn't long before my vow of abstinence began to slide.

I rationalized and promised myself to cut back on my drug use.

The love and joy that my daughter Rukiya brought into my life wasn't enough to elevate me to be a better place. Because of my lack of inner strength and determination, I eventually spiraled back into everyday drug use, which also severed the connection between me and Rukiya's mom, Lisa Allen-Sanders, and our kids from a previous marriage, Vicaious, and Latroy. Little Rukiya was no exception to the whole scheme of selfishness and misplaced priorities I had enshrined in my life. Even though I desired a life of sharing and loving with those that depended on me, I just wasn't ready at that time.

If it wasn't for my Mom and Dad spending time with Rukiya, even keeping her on some weekends, I may have lost all contact with my daughter. My parents did this while I traveled the country, stealing all along the way. There were times that I sent a small piece of change for Rukiya, but 99% of every dollar I stole went directly to the hands of drug dealers from coast to coast.

DENVER, COLORADO

My travels eventually landed me in Denver, Colorado, with a friend named Daniel Moore who we called Mook. Mook wanted to help me by introducing me to a city that could be more lucrative for my way of life. He was right. Denver was nice and I took every opportunity to make money. That, too, soon came to an end as I faced a murder charge brought against me. The only thing that I was guilty of was living the wrong lifestyle and protecting myself from an attack.

    It took two days before I was taken to court for arraignment. That's a formal procedure where your charges are read to you in court. I met my public defender, Robin Desmond, and her associates Fernando Freyre and Paul Radovich. They took me to a private room and introduced themselves. After the introductions, Robin asked me to tell her what happened. I refused, explaining to her that I wasn't going to say anything to anybody at this point because things were moving too fast for me and I needed time to think. Paul was visibly upset with my response and he wasted no time letting me know that I was lucky to have Robin as my attorney and, furthermore, she didn't have time to waste on me if I didn't want to tell her my story.

    Robin quickly eased the tension in the room by telling Paul to slow down, while also assuring me that she understood my reasoning and respected it. She then told me that she didn't need to hear my story about what happened.

    "I'm here for you, I want you to be free."

    I knew then that she was the one for me. After weeks of being incarcerated in the Denver

County Jail, Robin visited me. We talked about my case. At that time, she pointed out different aspects of the charge that gave her a good feeling about the outcome. We didn't talk long, but I felt good about her. I saw Robin a few more times at the jail after that, and each visit was encouraging.

Even though Robin was fighting hard to earn my freedom, my pursuit of drugs continued, even in jail and while my life was on the line. Yes, I found a hustle in jail that enabled me to have some occasional days of reconnection with my nemesis heroin. Eventually the occasional use was not enough, so I attempted to start a poker game against the wishes of the predominately Mexican population of the jail. The Mexicans already had a monopoly on poker, which was the most lucrative opportunity in the jail.

The Mexican inmates and I had gotten along well until then. Now, they came to me with warnings several times, with hopes that I would forego my plans to take over the poker game. I had one true partner with me, John Chambers. We were going into this together and he assured me that he was with me regardless of what I chose to do.

I knew in my head that we were about to enter a no-win situation, but I was blinded by the prospect of additional drugs. For that reason alone, I couldn't turn back. This eventually led to a knife fight involving me, one knife, John, and enough Mexicans to surround me three times. It didn't last long before I was stabbed in the side and they were still surrounding me with ill intent. I saw John throwing people from side to side in his attempt to keep folks off me.

At that moment everything stopped, the guards came in, and John, still standing by my side, asked me for the knife so that the guards wouldn't catch me with it. I was weak, just barely standing, but I remember telling him, "I ain't letting this knife go," and I didn't. If it hadn't been for John, I wouldn't be alive today.

When I awoke, I was in Denver County General Hospital with a punctured lung and diaphragm, barely alive. The doctor later told me that my heart had stopped, and they brought me back with a defibrillator. I remember my lawyer Robin at my bedside. She asked for my family's phone number. I hadn't told my mom and dad that I was locked up as I didn't want to let them down again. I most certainly didn't want them to know that I was laying on my death bed from a prison-gang knife fight, so I didn't give Robin the number then either.

After a day or so my doctor informed me that they needed to operate again because something was amiss. I told him I didn't want another surgery.

"If you don't get the surgery, you'll be dead before the day is over," he said.

"Let's do it then, Doc."

They performed the surgery, but I still wasn't out of danger. I was in a bad place, but I never felt like this was the end for me. Robin and Fernando popped up at my bedside. Again, she asked me to allow her to call my parents, pressing.

"Fred, they need to know what's happening with you."

I gave her their phone number, but I asked her not to tell my mom, even if she answered the phone. Tell my dad, I told her, and he'll tell Mom. She promised to do just that.

The next day my father arrived from St. Louis and stood at my bedside. His face was wonderful to behold and his presence breathed life into me. My father, ever the charmer, gave every nurse on the floor a rose with one request; save my son. The next surgery was successful and my recovery from that point was rapid. I was moved to a different building in the hospital to complete my recovery.

The recovery was fast but the pain lingered. The isolation from everyone bothered me the most. As it turned out, this time alone gave me an opportunity to read more and to start writing a book. Robin made it a point to provide me with reading material the whole time I was there, and I devoured every book she brought as rapidly as she brought them.

Her visits also allowed me the opportunity to share my writing with her, and to my surprise she seemed to be impressed. That in and of itself meant a lot to me because of the enormous respect and admiration I had for her. She went above and beyond the call of duty as an attorney. She must have known that I needed a real friend and that is exactly what she proved to be.

After months of recovering in the hospital, I was taken to court. I pled guilty to three years for involuntary manslaughter. With the jail time that I'd accumulated I wasn't in prison long. Upon my release, I stopped by Robin's office to give her one last thank you.

DRUGS WEREN'T FINISHED WITH ME

It wasn't long before I was back chasing that same old ghost of destruction. This eventually landed me in prison again, this time back in Missouri. It was there, in an institution called **Church Farm**, that I reconnected with an old friend called Big Stump. He introduced me to something that was instrumental in my recovery.

One day a lot of inmates were sitting in the corridor working on various pastimes. Some played cards or chess, others simply talked, sharing tall tales of unbelievable events from when they were free. But Big Stump was sitting at a table unloading pieces of wood from a box. I sat down with him and asked, "What are you doing?"

"I'm making a jewelry box," he answered.

"Out of this?"

"Yeah, out of this wood, this is cedar. Fred," he then asked, "are you tired yet?"

Damn! He must have been looking right through me because he knew and I knew exactly what he meant. He didn't wait for my answer. Instead offering, "I can show you something that will get you out of here."

He had my undivided attention. "What is that?" I asked.

"This wood, it will take you away if you let it."

I watched him work with this wood for twenty or thirty minutes, at which time I'd seen enough to know that this wasn't for me. I left Big Stump sitting there with his wood, and I didn't give our talk another thought.

A few nights later I lay awake in my bunk in a dormitory surrounded by about 200 men. My unhappiness and shame for my mostly unproductive life washed over me. I felt tears swell up in the corners of my eyes. I knew right then and there that I couldn't live with myself one minute longer. It was then that I began to pray, and I mean I ***prayed***! It wasn't loud enough for the ears of the mortals around me to hear, but it was plenty loud enough for God.

I went straight to God: no middleman, and no cause for people pleasing. This thing I'd gotten myself into was too serious and I just couldn't take it anymore. I made my case and I let God know that He would be hearing from me, all day, every day. I kept my word and through my continual prayer to lose the desire to use, He gave me the opportunity for a better life.

Weeks passed and I began to develop a sense of tranquility, and a greater desire to know myself. Once again, I ran into Stump sitting in the corridor, playing with that wood.

"Hey Stump, I see you're still at it."

"Yeah, Fred, this is what I do. Come on man, sit with me for a minute."

I did, and that minute turned into an hour, the hour turned into days. Before I knew it, I understood what Stump meant when he talked about leaving this place. I was gone. Though my body was encaged, my mind and spirit were free. I made clocks and jewelry boxes, not to mention the special orders that were heaped on me from inmates and even folks from the free world.

The time flew by and my parole hearing arrived. I'd never made parole before, so I wasn't looking for it then. But I wasn't giving up on it either. The day of my hearing, I made it a point to be well groomed and prepared to answer any question that was asked of me. After sitting in the hall, waiting my turn to go in front of the parole board, a man opened the doors and called my name. I noticed two men and a woman sitting behind a table.

"Have a seat Mr. Easter. My name is Penny.

Not Perfectly Divided

Penny Hubbard."

Penny then introduced the two men sitting on either side of her. No one other than Penny and I talked. She asked questions and I gave answers. This lasted about ten minutes.

"Okay, Mr. Easter, you can go," she said.

I expressed my appreciation to them all, along with my thanks for allowing me the opportunity to share my plans. I turned, walked toward the door, but before I could exit, she called to me.

"Mr. Easter, would you mind coming back for just a moment? I'd like to ask you another question."

"No, I don't mind at all." I responded. "How do you feel about house arrest?" She asked.

I paused momentarily, looked directly at her as if no one else existed. I then gave her my most sincere words of assurance.

"In the alley, on the roof, wherever you choose for me to be."

She smiled before saying, "You can go now, and you'll be hearing from us real soon."

Two days later I got my answer. In three weeks I was leaving the horrors of confinement. This was the first and only time I knew, without a doubt, that I would not be back. At last, they could take me off the register. I would no longer be a resident of these oversized tombs.

A BRAND-NEW ME

It was the summer of 1993. I left prison with the determination to reconstruct my life. Unlike many that returned to society with nowhere to live, I was blessed with a mom and dad that were overjoyed to lend me another helping hand. My fifteen-year-old niece, Amber, was living with them. And she, too, was thrilled to see me again. Not only that, but due to my sincere job search efforts, I landed a job. I sewed labels on shirts for a company whose most noted customer was Harley Davidson. I was able to excel in this position because of some prior training in prison for upholstery repair.

I was on a mission to work, save and prepare for a brighter future, and this job was a mere steppingstone in my quest to achieve just that. My sacrifices at this juncture of my life were drastic, but well thought out. I didn't spend a dime from my checks. I lived off the money that I made by cutting grass. And I was a *great* grass cutter.

My transportation back and forth to work was free because Amber let me use her bicycle. As it turned out, the bike wasn't too small because Amber was big for her age. I may have been a little cramped, but I enjoyed every minute of every day. This was *real* living.

I worked this way for almost a year and during this time I earned the trust and respect of my employer. Because of this I was instrumental in the hiring of other ex-convicts that desperately needed jobs. Just my word alone was enough to get them hired. I must admit, it felt good to know that my word meant something.

It was a Friday evening. I had just gotten paid and was taking my usual bike ride home on the street that cut through Calvary cemetery. I heard tires from a car squealing and looked around to see what was going on. To my surprise there were two cars, one chasing the other. They seemed to be going about 70 or 80 miles per hour, heading directly towards me. To make matters worse, there was a man standing up in the sunroof of the second car, shooting at the car in front. I could have sworn that I felt bullets whiz past my head. I jumped off the bike, rolled over and just missed getting run over by both cars. That was the end of my bike riding days.

The following day, I bought a used Cutlass Supreme and, while driving home, another car that looked just like mine pulled up along-side me.

"Hey, OG, you want to sell that car," one of the youngsters asked while checking out my car.

"I just bought it, man." I answered.

"Buy another one, I'll make it worth your while."

"Pull over," I told him.

We pulled over. There were three of them in the car. We talked momentarily, and then one of them flashed his bankroll. At that time, he made me an offer of more than a thousand dollars *more* than what I had paid for the car. I caught the bus home with that money in my pocket.

THE ENTREPRENUER

For the next six months I bought and sold cars, which enabled me to put enough money together to buy my first **LRA** house. **LRA** is a city agency that sells houses that have been taken from owners due to unpaid taxes. I put a crew of skilled workers together and I worked right alongside them, soaking up all the knowledge possible. I lived in the houses while I was remodeling them.

Things were turning around for me, but there was one important part of my life that was still broken. My daughter Rukiya had yet to give me access to her life. Don't get me wrong, we were spending time together, but she had her guard up, and I could understand why.

I vividly remember the day we talked in my car. It was a Wednesday and I pulled over, parked and began talking. I used every charm trick in the book to gain a real breakthrough into this 14-year-old daughter of mine. Nothing seemed to work. She was a hard nut to crack. I finally decided to bare my soul with honesty.

"Rukiya, there's something that you need to know."

She didn't respond, but I didn't need her to. I continued with my plea.

"I know it hasn't been easy for you, and most of the reason for that is because of me. What I'm about to say may be hard for you to understand, but I do hope that you'll hear me out."

I looked directly at her as she looked out the window, as if not really wanting to hear what I had to say. I knew in my heart, that this was the time—it was now or never for me to speak my peace.

"Rukiya, I've lived a selfish life, a life that didn't allow me to be right to myself, and if I couldn't be right to me, there's no way possible that I could be right to you or anybody else. But if you just give me one more chance, I promise that I'll never let you down again."

And I then finished with one last statement. "I'll be there for you and you can count on me. There's no need for you to give me an answer now, just think about it and remember, I love you."

We didn't do much more talking as I drove her home. She got out of the car and went into her house. I wasn't *that* nervous when I faced the parole board! I just knew that I had to have her in my life. Because she *is* me. I drove off, wondering when would be the next time that I would see her.

As it turned out, I didn't have to wait long. The very next day I got a call from her. She didn't say hi, nor did she use any other words of greetings. Instead, she simply said,

"I can spend the weekend with you. Do you want to pick me up?"

"I'll be there tomorrow evening to get you," I assured her.

I was floating on a cloud! I decided I had to pinch myself. I did, and it hurt! I knew then that it was true. She really wanted to spend time with me.

That was the most enjoyable weekend that I'd ever had in my life. With the help of my lady friend, Ernestine Scott, who knew how important my relationship with Rukiya was to me, I was able to begin forming a lasting friendship with my daughter that has grown stronger day by day. Since then she has married a great young man named Ivan Pargo, who is the son that I've always dreamed of having. They've blessed me with three grandchildren: Raven, Kamryn, Maddison and a great grandson named Chase. Rukiya and I still talk almost every day.

I eventually completed the work on my first house, sold it, bought others and sold some of those, too. I've started and operated several different businesses that have in turn created job opportunities for some that otherwise may have been unemployed.

Even though I haven't amassed a fortune I realize that my success is not gauged by money and things alone. Rather, it's in the positive difference that I've made to enrich the lives of others who might have needed a fresh start. I suppose that's why I've achieved so much satisfaction from the non-profit organizations that

I've been a part of.

My introduction as a participant to the world of non-profits began in 2013. My stepdaughter Kaya was at her wits end trying to save her son, Nico. He was getting into some type of trouble on a regular basis, which eventually led to legal issues. After she shared her heartfelt concerns with me, I, too, became worried. Even though I had lived a life as a thug, I still found myself unable to reach him. For this reason, I sought the advice from others. People who could reach him or put me in touch with people who could reach him.

My brother Harry connected me with an old friend of ours, Tommy T, who, in turn, introduced me to Sultan Muhammad. He headed an organization called Real Talk that had gained a well-respected reputation for turning around troubled kids. Nico and I attended our first meeting with Real Talk with Tommy T.

The meeting was held in the gymnasium of a grade school in University City. There seemed to be about forty kids, a few parents and a few devoted associates. To my surprise, most of the kids were relatively young. A few of them were only five or six. The amazing thing to me was the attentiveness that these youngsters showed to every speaker that addressed them. Brother Muhammad was certainly masterful with his words and his connection with these youngsters. They seemed to know he truly cared about them.

Nico wasn't sitting with me, but periodically I would take a quick glance at him just to get a feel for how he was receiving this message. He seemed to be watching and listening intently. After several speakers, Muhammad asked me if I would like to say a few words. My initial feeling was to take a pass on the offer because I always lacked the confidence for public speaking.

But as I looked around the room, the faces of these kids, especially Nico, would not allow me to be quiet. I spoke from the heart and everyone seemed to appreciate my message. A few let me know after the meeting.

We mingled and introduced ourselves while Nico and some of the other thirteen- or fourteen-year-old kids his age talked together. He seemed to enjoy himself and he confirmed my thoughts on the ride to his house by assuring me that he wanted to attend more meetings with Real Talk. As planned, we attended several more meetings at the school. But as it turned out, Nico's problems outweighed our desire to keep him on track. His days with Real Talk ended. I continued a little while longer, but I, too, soon discontinued the meetings.

But I had been bitten by the bug of helping kids. Because of this, at a later date my brother Harry and I began our own program named WORD, which stood for Working On Real Dreams. Yes, Harry was free and clean from the use of drugs too and he also wanted to make a positive difference in the lives of kids. Plus, he was always exceptional at connecting with anybody. Turns out he loved the interaction with these youngsters more than anything.

Once our commitment and dedication to our kids begin to bear fruit, good fortune seemed to follow us. We received help from Adolphus Pruitt, the President of the NAACP in the city of St. Louis. He in turn introduced us to Elston McCowan, another member of the NAACP, who had inroads into the public schools. McCowan worked vigorously to make a difference for the future of our youth in his ministry and at Walbridge School.

Harry and I eventually began mentoring youngsters at Walbridge Grade School and Blewit High School. Blewit was classified as a last chance opportunity for students. The school was founded by Judge Jimmy Edwards, a family court judge who has been instrumental in helping a countless number of our youth turn their lives around.

My brother Harry and I also had the good fortune to collaborate on another grassroots organization. Universal Advocates was comprised of several non-profit organizations that worked in mental health. The beauty in unifying these agencies was that we were able to connect people that needed help with trusted and capable professionals. The following are the names of the

organizations that were apart of Universal Advocates.
1. Art of Safety
2. Circle of Light Association
3. Churches of Scientology Disaster Response
4. Committed Caring Faith Communities
5. Delivered to Make a Difference
6. Foundation for a Drug Free World
7. Love Team Ministries INC.
8. Nothing Wasted
9. Restorative Justice Movement
10. Unmasking Suicide INC.
11. WORD; Working On Real Dreams
12. Youth For Human Rights International

    As rewarding as working with this group of committed and caring people has proven to be, the connections with others that followed has been just as gratifying. During the planning of our organization's first Mental Health Walk, Harry and I reconnected with an old friend. I first met Reverend Beins when I was sixteen, locked up in the city jail. At that time, he was the only link to help for some prisoners that had no one else to turn to. Harry knew Rev. Beins as well.

    After we talked with him on the phone, we met with him and other ministers at his church, The Lutheran Church of the Living Christ. We also met the parishioners at their church service. A few of us spoke at the church, which gave us the opportunity to share our vision of hope for the community. They shared our dream, and as a result, they offered help with our mission.

REPARATIONS BEGIN WITH FAMILIES

All struggles for justice begin with the family. This includes reparations as well. I am dismayed and bewildered when my people continue to focus exclusively on reparations. The more I research the wealth that we already possess, the greater my faith grows in our own transformative power. Self-reparation is already within our power. Before I go any further, I feel a need to quote to you the serenity prayer:

"God grant me the serenity to accept the things I cannot change,
Courage to change the things I can,
And wisdom to know the difference"

I see no harm in the asking for overdue reparations, go ahead and ask. But at the same time, we have the opportunity to treat ourselves right and not ask someone else to do it for us. A reparations plan, just like any other financial plan, would need to be well thought out with the right long-term goals in-mind. I emphasize this because we live in a world of instant everything, but this is not an instant process.

We must begin by creating an organization whose sole purpose is to act as a clearinghouse for united funds. These funds would be used to create our own learning institutions, create businesses, build a Black manufacturing base, and support lending institutions that are already supporting our community. Instead of our continuous blind support for those who have no desire to aid in our future wealth and power, we would slowly begin to lay the groundwork for a thriving business sector. We have educated experts in all areas that could implement each facet of this long overdue plan for our future wealth and power.

We have politicians, ministers, sports idols, and businessmen and women, who have the platform to recruit and spread the word. The funds will come from everyone who is able to contribute whatever they can afford. Keep in mind, nothing is free, not even freedom. We should know this more so than any other people on the planet. This is not the totality of our reparations plan, but it can be the start. Let's not forget that "thought" is the beginning of all plans. If we can think it, we can do it.

MY GREATEST APPRECIATION

While assessing the ups and downs in my life I now realize that all I've been through allows me to fully appreciate the courage and determination of young Black men and women. The fight for justice and equality by young people of all nationalities is infectious. Those of us who are still fighting for the dreams of our forefathers and mothers are pulled as if by a magnet toward this moment. Our forefathers' early sacrifices inspire us to do whatever is necessary to keep this ball going and gaining momentum as it rolls toward justice.

We have Black Lives Matter activists and young people from all walks of life participating in this movement with politicians, ministers, doctors, lawyers, professional athletes, underpaid fast food workers and others that have given up days of work and years of their life to work for their own and others' survival.

Too often we gauge the value of someone's sacrifice from a monetary point of view. This measurement is not fair, nor is it accurate. We have millions of people donating sums from bank accounts that they will never notice. These folks are greatly appreciated and needed, as are those who are giving up a day's work from a minimum wage job to lie in the street and get into good trouble.

These young protestors have contributed to a new self-awareness in me and a lot of other Americans. They have held a mirror to our inaction and convinced us to do more than give an occasional clap of the hands for the fight. For this reason, I wanted to seek out those on the front lines myself.

I participated in a peaceful protest on June 1, 2020, when marchers shut down Highway 40 in downtown St. Louis, Missouri. I didn't only protest, but I talked to fellow protesters, and it was like music to my ears to hear a unified message from every person.

"We're tired of being treated this way," they said. "We won't take it anymore, and we're going to stop it now." This was the repeated message, but not only that—it has become my message, too.

All parts in a movement are just as important as any other, and none will succeed without the support of every other part. I look forward to doing my piece for the movement by writing. My greatest opportunity to contribute in a meaningful way is by putting pen to paper. I've tried to shine a bit of light on the plight of this society through my own story and offer some solutions through the lens of my own life experience. I will write, but I'm also prepared to do more. I'll do what it takes. I'm more "all in" for this fight than I've ever been for anything in my life.

We all begin our journeys within our small, fractured family units, but thanks to young people in the US and all over the globe, we are beginning to imagine just how broad our human family extends. A lack of progress for some of us, is holding all of us back. It's time to stop dividing amongst ourselves and come together to advance the human cause.

Now is the time to rise and be counted. I am so very encouraged that this is the generation that may finally get the damned thing done. For my young family members, I want you to know I'm here for all of it! I'll be right there with you, ready to hand over that baton. We've carried it thus far, and we are proud and impressed by how you've run this next leg of the race so far. On to **FREEDOM, JUSTICE, AND EQUALITY**.

CONCLUSION

As imperfect as this Democracy may be, the Constitution and the balance of powers have always held firm in these United States of America. The aftermath of another four years of Donald Trump and a Republican controlled Senate could very well launch us into unending minority control of this country and affect the lives of all Americans for generations. All the gains made by people like Dr. Martin Luther King Jr., John Lewis, Rosa Parks and other freedom fighters could very well be lost. This somewhat free and just society may very well descend into an authoritarian regime like Russia, North Korea, Syria and other countries run by dictators with no regard for the rights of human beings.

This mistreatment will also catch the millionaires and billionaires who've stood idly by if they have any disagreements with the powerful one. And surely if any of Trump's most loyal supporters come to disagree with him, they, too, will feel the wrath. Therefore, no one should allow their temporary comfort zone to dissuade them from fighting for the rights of all. I hope, and pray that we don't follow this grim, yet very possible path, to a world unlike anything we've ever imagined for America. If this pursuit of earthly, infinite power is not checked, the human and civil rights of all people will be in jeopardy.

To make matters worse, Donald Trump and his lackeys are not the only virus that this country should be fighting. We also have the coronavirus that has claimed the lives of more than 200,000 Americans. Many of these deaths could have been avoided. Due to Donald Trump's efforts to paint a rosy picture of this crisis to enhance his election chances, coupled with the fact that he has no idea what he's doing and just down-right lacks empathy, we have put the lives of all Americans in danger during this pandemic.

I realize that the positions I take in this book will be contested, even by some closest to me. I only hope that these differences will serve to create dialogue rather than a deeper divide. I speak from the point of view of someone who has seen and felt the dagger of injustice on many sides. But through it all I cannot allow myself to cast the same shadow of unfairness on anyone else. If I was to do that, then I, too, would be just as guilty as those that have placed undue burdens on me. Based on my level of understanding, we spend wasteful hours of the day attempting to force others to live according to what we deem is right. Those wasteful hours would be better served working on self, which is a never-ending job for those aspiring to be their best.

<u>DON'T SWALLOW THE POISON PILL OF DIVISION!</u>

The Easter brothers with their daughters

Brother Charles and friends

Dad, Harry, Charles, and Joe

Classmates. Left to right, Rob, Derek, and Fred at Paula West's birthday party 8th grade

Fred and Joe with Mom

Fred and Wife

Fred, Ameriles, and Lawyers Robin and Fernando

My uncle, Luke Easter, started with the Cleveland Indians in 1949

My brother, Joe Easter El

Fred with brothers Joe, Daryl, Harry, and Dad

Fred at Free and Kaya's wedding

Luke Easter

The Penrose dance, 2018

Joe, Grandmother, Harry, Mom, and Dad

Fred with daughter, granddaughters and great-grandson

Highway 40 protest, St. Louis, Missouri, 2020

Protesting during the pandemic, 2020

Harry, Dr. Barry Black, and Fred

Fred, wife, son-in-law, daughter, granddaughters & great grandson

REFERENCES

Chapter I:

3. *Pocket Maya Angelou Wisdom: Inspirational Quotes and Wise Words from a Legendary Icon.* London: Hardie Grant Books, 2019.

4–6. Wallace, Willard M. "American Revolution." Encyclopædia Britannica. Encyclopædia Britannica, Inc., July 20, 1998. https://www.britannica.com/event/American-Revolution.

5. "First Enslaved Africans Arrive in Jamestown Colony." History.com. A&E Television Networks, August 13, 2019. https://www.history.com/this-day-in-history/first-african-slave-ship-arrives-jamestown-colony.

6. Passannante, August. "Henry Blair (1807–1860)." Black Past, January 30, 2020. https://www.blackpast.org/african-american-history/blair-henry-1807-1860/.

6. Bagley, Mary. "George Washington Carver: Biography, Inventions & Quotes." LiveScience. Purch, December 7, 2013. https://www.livescience.com/41780-george-washington-carver.html.

6. "Harriet Tubman." PBS. Public Broadcasting Service. Accessed December 23, 2020. https://www.pbs.org/wgbh/aia/part4/4p1535.html.

6–7. Deignan, Tom. "The Irish Hands That Built the Empire State Building." IrishCentral.com, May 4, 2020. https://www.irishcentral.com/roots/history/irish-empire-state-building.

7. The Kennedy's; w en.m.wikipedia.org>wiki>kenned. https://www.jfklibrary.org/learn/about-jfk/the-kennedy-family/joseph-p-kennedy

7–8. "Immigration and Relocation in U.S. History: A New Surge of Growth." The Library of Congress, n.d.

https://www.loc.gov/classroom-materials/immigration/german/new-surge-of-growth/.

10. "Destination America. When Did They Come?" PBS. Public Broadcasting Service, n.d. https://www.pbs.org/destinationamerica/usim_wn_noflash_5.html.

17–18. Lerer, Lisa, and Sydney Ember. "Examining Tara Reade's Sexual Assault Allegation Against Joe Biden." The New York Times. The New York Times, April 12, 2020. https://www.nytimes.com/2020/04/12/us/politics/joe-biden-tara-reade-sexual-assault-complaint.html.

22. Balsamo, Michael. "Over 3,000 Federal Inmates Released under Criminal Justice Overhaul." PBS. Public Broadcasting Service, July 19, 2019. https://www.pbs.org/newshour/nation/over-3000-federal-inmates-released-under-criminal-justice-overhaul.

24–26. Fausset, Richard. "Two Weapons, a Chase, a Killing and No Charges." The New York Times. The New York Times, April 26, 2020. https://www.nytimes.com/2020/04/26/us/ahmed-arbery-shooting-georgia.html.

31–32. O'Connor, Allison. "WILBERFORCE UNIVERSITY (1856–)." Black Past, January 10, 2020. https://www.blackpast.org/african-american-history/wilberforce-university-1856/.

32. "History of Tuskegee University." Tuskegee University, n.d. https://www.tuskegee.edu/about-us/history-and-mission.

36. Mettler, Katie, and Michael Scherer. "Obama Criticizes Nation's Leaders for Bungled Handling of Coronavirus Pandemic." The Washington Post. WP Company, May 17, 2020. https://www.washingtonpost.com/nation/2020/05/16/obama-commencement-speech-2020/.

45–48. Coates, Ta-Nehisi. "The Life Breonna Taylor Lived, in the Words of Her Mother." Vanity Fair, August 23, 2020. https://www.vanityfair.com/culture/2020/08/breonna-taylor.

49. "The Star-Spangled Banner." History.com. A&E Television Networks, September 28, 2017. https://www.history.com/topics/19th-century/the-star-spangled-banner.

CHAPTER II

58–59. Smith, James F. "Mandela Said to Reject Offer of Conditional Release." AP NEWS. Associated Press, February 10, 1985. https://apnews.com/article/b018ce150cd1ea7d457654e5e877c0fb.

60–61. "MLK Jr.'s Words of Freedom." Government Book Talk, January 14, 2016. https://govbooktalk.gpo.gov/.

62–63. Muhammad, Nafeesa. "The Nation of Islam's Economic Program, 1934–1975." Black Past, April 7, 2020. https://www.blackpast.org/african-american-history/the-nation-of-islams-economic-program-1934-1975/.

63. Editors. "Louis Farrakhan." Encyclopædia Britannica. Encyclopædia Britannica, inc., n.d. https://www.britannica.com/biography/Louis-Farrakhan.

63. "Noble Drew Ali." Encyclopædia Britannica. Encyclopædia Britannica, inc., n.d. https://www.britannica.com/biography/Noble-Drew-Ali.

66. Editors. "Syrian Civil War." Encyclopædia Britannica. Encyclopædia Britannica, Inc., July 6, 2011. https://www.britannica.com/event/Syrian-Civil-War.

66. Editors. "Egypt Uprising of 2011." Encyclopædia Britannica. Encyclopædia Britannica, Inc., February 11, 2011. https://www.britannica.com/event/Egypt-Uprising-of-2011.

CHAPTER III

69–70. Bird, Robert, and Frank Newport. "What Determines How Americans Perceive Their Social Class?" Gallup.com. Gallup, November 18, 2020. https://news.gallup.com/opinion/polling-matters/204497/determines-americans-perceive-social-class.aspx.

75–76. "Social Security Fifty Years Ago." Social Security History, n.d. https://www.ssa.gov/history/50ed.html.

79–80. "Background: Time for a New Approach?" CNN. Cable News Network, n.d. https://www.cnn.com/ALLPOLITICS/1997/gen/resources/infocus/welfare/background.html.

85–86. Roland, James. "The Pros and Cons of Obamacare." Healthline. Healthline Media, August 17, 2019. https://www.healthline.com/health/consumer-healthcare-guide/pros-and-cons-obamacare.

89–90. McDonald, Noreen, Ruth Steiner, Mathew Palmer, and Benjamin Lytle. "Quantifying the Full Costs of School Transportation." Active Living Research, March 2014. https://activelivingresearch.org/quantifying-full-costs-school-transportation.

90. Davis, Jen. "The Disadvantages of Taking a School Bus." How to Adult, September 22, 2017. https://howtoadult.com/the-disadvantages-of-taking-a-school-bus-12500534.html.

94–95. Kulis, Stephen, Flavio Francisco Marsiglia, Diane Sicotte, and Tanya Nieri. "Neighborhood Effects on Youth Substance Use in a Southwestern City." Sociological perspectives: SP: official publication of the Pacific Sociological Association. U.S. National Library of Medicine, 2007. doi:10.1525/sop.2007.50.2.273

95. Hinders, Dan. "Poverty and Addiction Relationship." St. Joseph Institute for Addiction, September 11, 2019. https://stjosephinstitute.com/understanding-the-relationship-between-poverty-and-addiction/.

CHAPTER IV

123–124. Itkowitz, Colby. "At Memorial Service, John Lewis's Family Urges Americans to Keep His Legacy Alive." The Washington Post. WP Company, July 26, 2020. https://www.washingtonpost.com/powerpost/at-memorial-service-john-lewiss-family-urges-americans-to-keep-his-legacy-alive/2020/07/25/845b273a-ce72-11ea-bc6a-6841b28d9093_story.html.

CHAPTER V POLITICAL DIVIDE

117–118. O'Connell, Jonathan, Steven Rich, and Peter Whoriskey. "Public Companies Received $1 Billion in Stimulus Funds Meant for Small Businesses." The Washington Post. WP Company, May 6, 2020. https://www.washingtonpost.com/business/2020/05/01/sba-ppp-public-companies/.

124. Savage, Charlie, Eric Schmitt, and Michael Schwirtz. "Russia Secretly Offered Afghan Militants Bounties to Kill U.S. Troops, Intelligence Says." The New York Times. The New York Times, June 26, 2020.

https://www.nytimes.com/2020/06/26/us/politics/russia-afghanistan-bounties.html.

134–135. Ogbar, Jeffrey O.G. "The FBI's War on Civil Rights Leaders." The Daily Beast. The Daily Beast Company, January 16, 2017. https://www.thedailybeast.com/the-fbis-war-on-civil-rights-leaders?ref=author.

CHAPTER VI GENDER DIVIDE

137. "Women's Suffrage." History.com. A&E Television Networks, October 29, 2009. https://www.history.com/topics/womens-history/the-fight-for-womens-suffrage.

138. "Ida B. Wells-Barnett." Encyclopædia Britannica. Encyclopædia Britannica, Inc., n.d. https://www.britannica.com/biography/Ida-B-Wells-Barnett.

139. "Alice Paul." Biography.com. A&E Networks Television, July 9, 2020. https://www.biography.com/activist/alice-paul.

140. Michals, Debra. "Shirley Chisholm." National Women's History Museum, 2015. https://www.womenshistory.org/education-resources/biographies/shirley-chisholm.

148. "Women Who Fought for the Vote." History.com. A&E Television Networks, October 14, 2009. https://www.history.com/topics/womens-history/women-who-fought-for-the-vote-1.

148–149. Gandhi, Lakshmi. "5 Black Suffragists Who Fought for the 19th Amendment—And Much More." History.com. A&E Television Networks, August 4, 2020. https://history.com/news/black-suffragists-19th-amendment.

149. Knight, Stephanie. "JOSEPHINE ST. PIERRE RUFFIN (1842–1924)." Black Past, January 18, 2007. https://www.blackpast.org/african-american-history/ruffin-josephine-st-pierre-1842-1924/.

149. Sisson, Wade. "The Titanic's Final Days: A Daily Timeline." The Denver Post. The Denver Post, March 16, 2012. https://www.denverpost.com/2012/03/16/the-titanics-final-days-a-daily-timeline/.

149–150. Waxman, Olivia B. "Myths About the 19th Amendment and Women's Suffrage Debunked." Time. Time, August 18, 2020. https://time.com/5879346/19th-amendment-facts-myths/.

151–152. Edmondson, Catie. "DeJoy Defends Postal Changes as Trump Continues to Attack Voting by Mail." The New York Times. The New York Times, August 24, 2020. https://www.nytimes.com/2020/08/24/us/politics/louis-dejoy-post-office-hearing.html.

152. Simmons-Duffin, Selena. "How the Supreme Court's Ruling May Affect the Trump Administration's Actions." NPR. NPR, June 15, 2020. https://www.npr.org/2020/06/15/877585259/how-the-supreme-courts-ruling-may-affect-the-trump-administrations-actions.

159. Duignan, Brian. "Rosa Parks, the Montgomery Bus Boycott, and the Birth of the Civil Rights Movement." Encyclopædia Britannica. Encyclopædia Britannica, Inc., n.d. https://www.britannica.com/story/mother-of-the-civil-rights-movement.

159–160. "Nannie Helen Burroughs (U.S. National Park Service)." National Parks Service. U.S. Department of the Interior, n.d. https://www.nps.gov/people/nannie-helen-burroughs.htm.

160. "Who Was Ella Baker?" Ella Baker Center for Human Rights, December 18, 2020. https://ellabakercenter.org/who-was-ella-baker/.

160–161. Bakare, Lanre. "Angela Davis: 'We Knew the Role of the Police Was to Protect White Supremacy'." The Guardian. Guardian News and Media, June 15, 2020. https://www.theguardian.com/us-news/2020/jun/15/angela-davis-on-george-floyd-as-long-as-the-violence-of-racism-remains-no-one-is-safe.

161. Rivas, Rebecca. "Cori Bush Heads to Congress after Celebrated Win in Missouri." Columbia Missourian, November 24, 2020. https://www.columbiamissourian.com/news/state_news/cori-bush-heads-to-congress-after-celebrated-win-in-missouri/article_4220c07c-29c2-11eb-8ec8-abc5e42e2d82.html.

161–163. Dovere, Edward-Isaac. "Why Joe Biden Picked Kamala Harris." The Atlantic. Atlantic Media Company, September 11, 2020. https://www.theatlantic.com/politics/archive/2020/08/why-biden-picked-harris/615100/.

CHAPTER VII THE POWER OF SPORTS IN POLITICS

165–166. ROD. "Black History Month: Day 12–Jesse Owens Goes to Germany and Finds Brotherhood." Travelbox Adventures, February 20, 2017. https://travelboxadventures.com/2017/02/13/jesse-owens/.

167. Waleik, Gary. "A History of Memorable Celtics Trades." A History of Memorable Celtics Trades | WBUR News. WBUR, March 13, 2012. https://www.wbur.org/news/2012/03/13/history-celtics-trades.

167. Waleik, Gary. "Finally: Bill Russell Statue Finds A Home in Boston." Finally: Bill Russell Statue Finds A Home in Boston | Only A Game. WBUR, July 14, 2011. https://www.wbur.org/onlyagame/2011/07/14/bill-russell.

167-168. Erin. "How the Black Power Protest at the 1968 Olympics Killed Careers." History.com. A&E Television Networks, February 22, 2018. https://www.history.com/news/1968-mexico-city-olympics-black-power-protest-backlash.

168. Klein, Christopher. "Muhammad Ali vs. the United States of America." History.com. A&E Television Networks, April 28, 2017. https://www.history.com/news/muhammad-ali-vs-the-united-states-of-america.

169. Proctor, Clare. "Jacob Blake Handcuffed to Hospital Bed, Father Says." Times. Chicago Sun-Times, August 28, 2020. https://chicago.suntimes.com/2020/8/27/21404463/jacob-blake-father-kenosha-police-shooting-hospital-bed-handcuffs.

171–172. Helin, Kurt. "NBA Players Who Don't Want to Play in Restart Reportedly Will Not Be Punished." ProBasketballTalk | NBC Sports, June 10, 2020. https://nba.nbcsports.com/2020/06/10/nba-players-dont-want-to-play-not-punished/.

www.ingramcontent.com/pod-product-compliance
Lightning Source LLC
Chambersburg PA
CBHW070730160426
43192CB00009B/1381